one woman's search for authentic love

# promises in the dark

beth jones

*Promises In The Dark: One Woman's Search For Authentic Love*
© 2014 Beth Jones

Published by:

Refreshing Waters
P. O. Box 452
Butler, MO 64730
United States of America

Cover Design by Christine E. Dupre
Back cover photo by Leah Jones

Manufactured in the United States of America. All rights reserved. No part of this book may be reproduced in any form or by any electronic or mechanical means, including information storage or retrieval systems, without the express permission in writing by the author and/or publisher. Brief quotations in printed reviews are permissible. For more information, go to http://www.bethjones.net.

This is a work of nonfiction. The events are portrayed to the best of Beth Jones' memory. While all the stories in this book are true, some names and identifying details have been changed to pseudonyms to protect the privacy of the people involved.

Unless otherwise designated, Scripture quotations are from the Holy Bible, New International Version®, NIV®. Copyright ©1973, 1978, 1984, 2011 by Biblica, Inc.™ Used by permission of Zondervan. All rights reserved worldwide. www.zondervan.com. The "NIV" and "New International Version" are trademarks registered in the United States Patent and Trademark Office by Biblica, Inc.™

Scripture quotations marked "MSG" or "The Message" are taken from The Message. Copyright 1993, 1994, 1995, 1996, 1996, 2000, 2001, 2002. Used by permission of NavPress Publishing Group.

Scripture quotations marked "ESV" are from The Holy Bible, English Standard Version® (ESV®) Copyright © 2001 by Crossway, a publishing ministry of Good News Publishers. All rights reserved. ESV Text Edition: 2007.

Scripture quotations marked "NKJV" are from The New King James Version®. Copyright © 1982 by Thomas Nelson, Inc. Used by permission. All rights reserved.

Scripture quotations marked "KJV" are taken from the Holy Bible, King James Version, Cambridge, 1769.

Scripture quotations marked "NASB" are taken from the New American Standard Bible, Copyright 1960, 1962, 1963, 1971, 1972, 1973, 1975, 1977, 1995 by The Lockman Foundation. Used by permission.

Scriptures taken from The Contemporary English Standard Version®. The Good News Bible© 1994 published by the Bible Societies/HarperCollins Publishers Ltd UK, Good News Bible© American Bible Society 1966, 1971, 1976, 1992. Used with permission.

Scripture quotations marked "NLT" are taken from the Holy Bible, New Living Translation, copyright 1996. Used by permission of Tyndale House Publishers, Inc., Wheaton, Illinois 60189. All rights reserved.

Scripture quotations marked "TLB" or "The Living Bible" are taken from The Living Bible [computer file] / Kenneth N. Taylor. electronic ed. Wheaton : Tyndale House, 1997, c1971 by Tyndale House Publishers, Inc. Used by permission. All rights reserved.

Scriptures taken from The Amplified Bible., Copyright © 1954, 1958, 1962, 1964, 1965, 1987 by The Lockman Foundation. Used by permission.

ISBN 10: 06922 30211
ISBN 13: 978-0-692-23021-3

# Medical Disclaimer

This book is not intended as a substitute for the advice of physicians, professional therapists, counselors, psychologists, or psychiatrists. It shall not take the place of a medical or psychiatric evaluation, diagnosis, and/or treatment. The information shared in this book is my personal experience and are facts gathered during extensive research. This information does not constitute medical, professional counseling or psychiatric advice and the accuracy of the information is not guaranteed. Furthermore, individuals are recommended to seek professional medical, counseling or psychiatric assistance in the event they are suffering mental health and/or medical conditions.

# About the Author

Beth Jones is an international Speaker, Author, and Coach. She empowers women and offers refreshing hope to them through the power of personal story. Her mission is equipping women to use their gifts for God, doing what they love and prospering in every area of life. You can find out more about Beth's keynote women's conference speaking and services at http://www.bethjones.net. To contact Beth directly, email her at elizabethdjones@gmail.com.

# Testimonials

*Promises In The Dark* is Beth's life story of warfare and triumph. She shares parts of her life that not many would admit, only for the glory of God. Beth is brilliant in showing that no matter how hard or terrifying life may get, God is always present with unconditional love that no human can give. *Promises In The Dark* enlightens you with the power of God's Word and promises that confronts all darkness.

*Rochelle Valasek, Doctor of Divinity, Speaker/Author/Spiritual Health Coach, www.RochelleValasek.com*

Beth's book *Promises In The Dark* is a powerful testimony to the love of God for His children. Beth has managed to drag the dark secrets and sins from her past into the amazing light of Christ's forgiveness and faithfulness. She shows us that God is patient and merciful; He extends His hope to those of us in the grips of sin. God's promises transcend what the world offers us; in Christ alone we find the unconditional love and acceptance that validates our worth and value. Beth's book is an honest look at how the trauma of abuse, sin and deception kept her captive. Thank God the story doesn't end there, for her or any of us. A very worthwhile read for anyone who struggles to overcome the world's lies and wants to reach for the promises of God.

*Maria Willis, MS, Clinical Psychology*

Beth Jones is a living example of how God can take the most tragic circumstances in life and turn them around for His glory. *Promises In The Dark* is an inspiring true testimony revealing how hollow and devastating the world's promises can be compared to the faithful and everlasting promises of God. It is a beautifully written, transparent, autobiographical work that will encourage you to evaluate and break free from the false worldly promises of your past and inspire you to seek God and His true promises for your life.

*Kimberly Weber, Jacksonville, FL, Homeschooling mom and Homeschool Portfolio Evaluator*

Beth reveals the many false "promises in the dark" she believed as she searched for love in all the wrong places. She shares her hurts, pains, and life choices with truthfulness and transparency. For any woman who is seeking freedom from the impact of childhood abuse, abortion, or adultery, Beth's testimony of hope can also be yours. *Promises In The Dark* is summed up in Beth's statement, "God also whispers you promises in the dark, but His promises are the real thing."

*Karen Wells, M.Div., Therapist, Author, Speaker, Radio Host, Karis Counselling Services, www.mybestlifepossible.com*

When I first heard Beth Jones speak, I knew I had come in contact with a woman who was overflowing with godly wisdom and fire for the Lord. I wouldn't have guessed then that she has suffered so many dark trials, beginning in childhood. I am now honored to call Beth my friend, and to continue learning from and being encouraged by her. This book, *Promises In The Dark*, is Beth's testimony to how God can and does give beauty for ashes, strength for fear, gladness for mourning, and a heart of praise for despair. He lifts those who mourn and makes them "Oaks of righteousness" for the display of His splendor. Thank you Beth, for following His lead and sharing your story with us. I pray that God will lead many to healing as a result of reading your testimony."

*Beth Cranford, wife, homeschooling mom, speaker, blogger, www.BethCranford.com*

# Dedication

For our three beautiful, precious daughters, Heather, Eden, and Leah. Weeping may last through the night, but joy comes in the morning. (Psalm 30: 5)

God has seen all my tears and your tears through life's great hardships and pain, and He is our Healer and Restorer. Jesus loves you so much. He is Authentic Love. As He told Peter on the beach after His resurrection, follow Him. (John 21:18-19)

I love you so much.

## A special thanks...

A special thanks to my so-hard-working, "man of God, fire" husband Ray, our beautiful, precious daughters Heather, Eden, and Leah, my beloved sister Maria, my faithful, powerful intercessor team members, my anointed mastermind partners Shelley Valasek and Tony Robinson, my encouraging, filled-with-wisdom prayer/accountability partner, Doreen Penner, our servant-heart, loving pastors Dave and Ruth Christian, my small group members Dan, Liz, Anita, David, Denise, Penny, my precious family, my daily strength online and offline friends, all who encouraged me when I wanted to just quit and who spurred me on to finish this book. Christine Dupre, you do amazing, beautiful work. I LOVE my cover! Hanne Moon, you are incredible. Christine and you are a huge answer to prayer. Thank you for believing in me, despite myself. Jesus, deep calls to deep. I love you all.

# contents

**Introduction**
*A Broken Vessel*
1

**Chapter 1**
*Promises: The Fairy Godmother*
7

**Chapter 2**
*Abuse: Cinderalla by the Ashes*
19

**Chapter 3**
*Abortion: You Can't Go to the Ball*
73

**Chapter 4**
*Education: Cinderella Sweeping the Floor*
123

**Chapter 5**
*Adultery: Other Dreams*
**137**

**Chapter 6**
*Marriage: Dancing With the Prince*
155

**Chapter 7**
*Just Jesus: The Glass Slipper*
175

**Call To Action**
185

**Endnotes**
189

**Resources**
203

**About the Author**
209

# Introduction
# a broken vessel

Has your heart been broken?

Mine, too. Writing is a gift and tool God has given me to help heal from the pain.

It's been prophesied over me by several different people that I would write many books in my life. I love writing. I've been writing since I was a child. As a teen, I poured out my heart in my diary about dreams of marriage, children, and my own beautiful home one day, or I'd write fiction short stories in my childhood bedroom, sitting on the curved seat of the antique, mirrored dresser (pictured), using the drawer top as my desk.

After I finished a chapter, I'd stuff the notebook papers into the drawer and later my younger sister Maria would sneak into my room to read them. I'd find out and get mad that she violated my privacy, and we'd fight. We'd yell at each other, I'd throw her Barbie doll, and she'd scratch me with her long nails and pull my hair.

I should have been flattered that she wanted to read my writing. Now she is one of my best friends and biggest fans, cheering me on to the "Writing Success" finish line, just like I encouraged and motivated her (it was more like, "Get off your butt, stop making excuses and do it!") to go to college at mid-life and earn her B.A. and then her master's degree in psychology to become a therapist, working with abused children. (She's had years of practice counseling me with depression, anxiety, and other issues anyway!)

I've authored six books so far, none of which have seen great worldly "success"...but I write on to please the audience of One, my God and King, and to encourage others with what God has put into my hands for His glory, this writing gift.

This is one book that I'd rather not write. An autobiography seems self-indulgent, too exposing of my sins, and, worst, *boring*—the cardinal sin of a writer. Maybe you'll even think I'm crazy. Maybe you'll stop liking me and have nothing more to do with me. I hope you won't, but I'll take the risk to find my voice and speak truth.

> "Those things we stuff, try so hard to ignore, they are the very things begging for release—the things that hold the promise of hope, the flame of freedom."[1]

One night, God gave me the title of this book and spoke to my heart to write it, so I must obey. I've had major writing resistance with this book, more so than any other I've written. I've prayed a lot and asked God what to write and what NOT to include in this book, wrestling with Him as Jacob did, wanting His blessing. Wrestling with myself.

> "O afflicted one, storm-tossed and not comforted, I will set your stones in antimony[2], and lay your foundations with sapphires."[3]

Afflicted and storm-tossed, yep, that's me alright. This is a scripture God has spoken to me many times.

It's been very painful to write this story, baring myself naked in these pages for the world to see. Some people have questioned me about writing this book, because I share such private things—things that probably will hurt Ray, our children, my family, and friends.

Exposing myself in this book is sort of like going to a California beach with all the hot, skinny, gloriously golden-tan girls, and there you are in your one-piece, black bathing suit, trying to cover your very imperfect body. The hot chicks and hunks on the beach either ignore you as if you're invisible or desperately want you to put your clothes back on. Your body is indecent. It makes people squirm, so uncomfortable—yet they still gawk and stare curiously.

Yes, that is the way I feel with this book. Very vulnerable and scary.

But I am God's sheep; I hear Jesus the Shepherd's voice and I have to obey to write. And I'm not trying to hurt anyone with this book. God knows my heart of broken hearts.

I've needed God's wisdom and discernment as I've strained to work on it, my turbulent soul poised, my fingers hesitating at the laptop keys. The careful, prudent, nice-mannered editor in my head gasping for air, "Don't write that! It's embarrassing!" has to die violently. Yet I don't want to just purge onto the page everything bad that I've done or that has happened to me, but to write what builds up and encourages others.

There's many more terrible things that have happened to me which I don't share in this book—not because I am trying to keep more secrets, but because I don't believe those details are necessary for the edification of the Body of Christ for this book. Nor do they fit in with the premise of this book: God's promises versus the world's promises.

Maybe those other things will be in another book that I'll write someday. I have many more books inside of me. I'm discovering that the more I share the "bad stuff" in my life, the freer in Christ I become. When we are transparent as glass, our hands, and our hearts open, expectant and trusting solely in God, we have nothing to hide. Yet I remember:

> "Let no corrupt communication proceed out of your mouth, but that which is good to the use of edifying, that it may minister grace unto the hearers."[4]

I want what I write to be relevant and a timely word in due season[5], to have a point and to give others hope. To show off Jesus, not to glorify myself or the enemy's activities.

I've had to push past the fear of being judged and rejected, worrying about what others would think, including my own family of origin, my husband and our children, my extended family, our friends, and my business peers.

I'm willing to risk judgment, rejection, and alienation, even from those I love dearly, for exposing the darkness of my past, if it will help just one person to find the limitless power and light of God's unconditional love and forgiveness.

I believe God will use the message within these pages to speak life and truth to many women who know the pain of childhood abuse, abortion, and adultery, to set them free.

More importantly, the purpose of me writing this book is to share that while the world promises you many wonderful things, it often comes up empty; but God's promises are true and forever. He is faithful. You can always count on Him and His promises.

I am simply God's *Message in a Bottle*[6], His treasure in a fragile clay jar[7].

My prayer is that you'll find complete healing through Jesus Christ, and then allow Him to use your pain for Him. God makes beautiful things out of brokenness.

In the words of Gene Edwards, author of *A Tale of Three Kings*:

> "David was caught in a very uncomfortable position; however, he seemed to grasp a deep understanding of the unfolding drama in which he had been caught. He seemed to understand something that few of even the wisest men of his day understood. Something that in our day, when men are wiser still, even fewer understand. And what was that? God did not have - but wanted very much to have - men and women who would live in pain. **God wanted a broken vessel.**"[8]

PROMISES IN THE DARK

# Chapter 1
# promises:
# the fairy godmother

*"This is beautiful," I said, ignoring the shop window to trace the gleaming stone walls fronting another boutique.*

*"You know what's funny?" Jacob asked. He didn't wait for my answer. "You can see beauty in everything, except for yourself."*

Justina Chen, *North of Beautiful*

"You're too beautiful to be treated this way. Your husband should treat you so much better. If you were my wife, I'd treat you the way you deserve." The male psychiatric technician smiled, his eyes sweeping over my body as I lay on the hospital bed, too distressed to sleep.

It was night, and I was shrouded in fear and that dark beast, depression, ravaged my mind. I was on suicide watch, being observed carefully by the staff and the psych tech was on duty that night. He was the technician who initially checked me into the hospital, taking away "sharps" (anything with a sharp edge that could be used to cut or hurt a patient) or any chemical products that could be harmful or fatal if ingested.

Tears streamed down my face as I talked with him about the turmoil and the constant strife in my less than one-year-old marriage. Shortly before coming to this hospital, I'd made the second serious attempt to end my life, overdosing on anti-depressants and anti-anxiety meds to end the pain.

In that attempt after I called him to say goodbye, Ray found me drowsy in my car, with a suicide note on the seat apologizing to him and Heather. He had frantically run miles to find me, led only by my vague directions of my whereabouts and the Holy Spirit's wisdom. Terrified when he found me and seeing the suicide note, he hurriedly drove me to the hospital where I had my stomach pumped of the drugs.

The hospital released me the next day, thinking it was just a cry for help since I'd called Ray before the overdose, and I was physically unharmed and seemed perfectly normal to the staff the next morning. I just wanted the emotional pain to stop. While it may have been a cry for help, this attempt was more dangerous than my first attempt since it involved prescription drugs.

The first time I'd tried to commit suicide, I attempted to slash my wrists with a purse mirror while a volunteer patient at a hospital. I'd quietly broken my compact mirror into pieces, and tried to cut my wrists in my room. No matter how hard I tried, though, I wasn't able to penetrate my white skin deeply enough and had been discovered by a staff person—God's protection and intervention to save my life.

Thin rivers of red blood seeped from my wrists, but it was my heart that was really bleeding. I just wanted the pain to stop. I was afraid I was going to wind up succeeding at killing myself, and then what would happen to my daughter Heather? Yes, Ray would take care of and love her, but it would devastate her life.

At this new hospital, massive doses of anti-depressant and anti-anxiety medications, prescribed by my new psychiatrist for quick intervention, further clouded my anguished mind. Hurt, disassociated from life's past traumas and present pain, and heavily drugged, I felt as if I weren't able to see or find my way through the confusion. It was eerily like Scarlett O'Hara's dream in the fog, where she was running from something fearful, not knowing what it was, or who or what her safe haven was.

> "And something terrifying was pursuing her and she was running till her heart was bursting, running in a thick swimming fog, crying out blindly seeking that nameless, unknown haven of safety that was somewhere in the mist around her."[9]

My life was spinning rapidly out of control with the additional stresses of a new marriage, severe financial struggles when Ray became unemployed shortly after we married, caring full-time for my toddler, hyperactive stepdaughter Eden, and playing referee between Eden and my daughter Heather, who constantly argued.

A grey, long-haired, Persian kitten named Takara, which Ray brought home that I at first thought was adorable, had become a wild feral cat, clawing our family's hands bloody and clawing and biting my beloved registered, purebred Siamese cat Torie.

At night, Takara would attack my bare feet as I slept, frightening me out of sleep—which I already had problems with due to insomnia. Many nights, I'd stay awake all night long, reading books, writing in my journal, trying to talk to Ray who patiently indulged me. His patience has worn paper thin through the 21 years of our marriage. At times we bite, we devour one another; our souls cry for grace to endure the marriage.

The next day, he would be exhausted and I'd sleep for several hours. Side effects of insomnia include depression, lack of concentration, irritability, and fatigue.[10]  We were both worn out. I dreaded the night, and often felt panicky during the daytime.

The tiny, cute apartment which had suited me as a single mom that I shared with Heather was becoming claustrophobic and a source of anxiety, when Ray and Eden moved in with their clothes, furniture, and other belongings. Everything was closing in on me, like an unstoppable freight train crash. I quickly found out that Ray was a hoarder and threw almost nothing away. It caused years of strife and is still to this day a sore point between us.

I kept our home immaculately clean, but the low-income apartment complex began to have a problem with roaches from the other tenants, which triggered great fear in me. Today our kids jokingly refer to that apartment as "the roach motel." The roaches terrified me and made me jump and scream.

My marriage was quickly unraveling with our increasing financial problems, and I felt as if I too were unraveling.

I wanted to escape life, but couldn't find any safe, peaceful haven. I couldn't find my compass, my "true north."

I'd hoped this new hospital was the answer to heal me. My therapist and my psychiatrist helped me to be admitted as a voluntary patient at a hospital that was miles away from my home and my family, to get the best possible psychiatric help in the country for my increasing suicidal ideation, cutting , depression, nightmares, and panic attacks.

The chief-of-staff psychiatrist was well known for his effective treatment of childhood sexual abuse and incest victims. I thought I'd finally get the healing I needed from him at this hospital, after five years of weekly counseling for my childhood abuse and other traumatic life events.

With a diagnosis of PTSD (Post Traumatic Stress Disorder), major depressive order, and panic disorder, I was the textbook example of a childhood abuse survivor. The psychological effects of the abuse were affecting everyone around me and everything in my life.

> *You can suffer the pain of change or suffer remaining the way you are.*
> *~ Joyce Meyer ~*

My therapist was deeply concerned about my recent two suicide attempts, and afraid of a third one, that I might not survive. He felt that the physical distance between Ray and me while I was at the hospital for a short period of time might stabilize me emotionally and help us both to get a much needed break. He wrote the necessary letters for my voluntary admission to the hospital. The decision to go to this hospital would be one of the biggest mistakes of my life.

As I looked up desperately at the technician's eyes in the dark, I saw a glitter of something besides a smile...lust and something sinister. I brushed away the fear, my ego longing for his affirming words. He had called me beautiful. *Beautiful* stuck in my head. I couldn't hear it enough. *You deserve to be treated better. I'd treat you better.*

*Promises in the dark.*

Patients at this hospital were given passes over a period of time by doctors if they fully complied with their treatment (like a reward). This technician offered to take me out shopping and dining when I earned my passes, knowing I was married and that Ray was at home with our children in another state.

On the pass, the technician gave me a $100 bill as a "gift," which

I used to buy a black coat at a mall. He took me out to eat. Then he took me to his apartment, plied me with alcohol (well aware that I was heavily medicated on anti-depressant and anti-anxiety medications, which could have killed me), and had sex with me. He took me on a second pass, with very similar circumstances happening, including the alcohol and sex. He often told me how beautiful I was, saying I should leave Ray and that he wanted to marry me.

*Promises in the dark.*

Ray first found out about this situation from a female patient who befriended me quickly at the hospital and had been released to go home. When she became aware that I was with this technician, she called Ray, very concerned, and told him that I was with "a very bad, dangerous man." She told Ray that she was afraid this man was going to hurt me.

Ray, who knew nothing of this situation prior to her call and was scared out of his wits and heartbroken, called the hospital, threatening a big lawsuit if they didn't find my whereabouts immediately and fire and prosecute the technician.

The hospital staff realized they had a serious liability lawsuit on their hands. Ray, terrified that my life was at risk, called the police to file a missing persons report. The technician brought me back to the hospital several hours later, and his employment was instantly terminated. The police began investigating him.

I was admitted to the hospital again and after a short stay, I was released into Ray's care. Back home, we filed a lawsuit against the hospital and the technician for patient abuse and severe negligence of patient care.

The police detectives' thorough years of investigation of the technician exposed a pattern of similar abusive behavior: this man had a history of having sex at his apartment with female patients who had been sexually abused in childhood, while working at this hospital and at previous other places he had worked. He was a predator.

Ray and I settled out of court after years of intensely stressful, drawn-out litigation. What this man did to us has haunted our lives.

This man's sexual abuse of me nearly destroyed my sanity and my marriage. I left the hospital in a far worst psychological state of mind that when I first came there. God has done amazing, miraculous healing in my life since then, but there are deep scars. Ray and I are still trying to heal today. We've been on the verge of divorce for years, never fully recovering.

*Promises in the dark.*

Maybe you, too, have been told promises in the dark. Maybe you were promised love, if you gave someone sex. Maybe some man or woman gave you false promises in your relationship, however short or long it was, and broke your heart.

Maybe you were told these promises as a child: *If you'll just be good and quiet, and not tell anyone what we're doing, I will buy you candy... give you money... take you to that special place you want to go to this weekend...always love you.* Or you or someone you loved were threatened to be harmed or killed if you did tell.

Maybe you were given the promise that an abortion would make all your problems go away.

PROMISES IN THE DARK

Maybe you have been given the promise that if you just work hard and long enough, and do what the online gurus tell you to do, buying their $5,000 or $10,000 program, you finally will have success...wealth...international travel...a vacation on an exotic island with a fruity drink with the little umbrella in it...the life you've always dreamed of.

Promises in the dark that you grasp for, but can't hold onto. Empty promises like a barren or miscarrying womb. Promises that render you unfulfilled, that leave you still looking for something or Someone.

Promises that devastate yours—and others'—lives. Promises which have no truth in them, or partial truths, to deceive you. Promises you can't count on.

There is One whose promises you can trust. His name is God. He is Faithful and True.[12] He isn't like men or women; He doesn't lie.[13] God won't ever leave you or abandon you.[14]

He won't ever forget you. You are written on the palms of His hands.[15] Even if you sin, and especially when you sin, God stretches out His arms of Love and Forgiveness to you and takes you back, as we see in the story of the woman caught in adultery:

> Jesus went across to Mount Olives, but he was soon back in the Temple again. Swarms of people came to him. He sat down and taught them.
>
> The religion scholars and Pharisees led in a woman who had been caught in an act of adultery. They stood her in plain sight of everyone and said, "Teacher, this woman was caught red-handed in the act of adultery. Moses, in the Law, gives orders to stone such persons. What do you say?"

They were trying to trap him into saying something incriminating so they could bring charges against him.

Jesus bent down and wrote with his finger in the dirt. They kept at him, badgering him. He straightened up and said, "The sinless one among you, go first: Throw the stone." Bending down again, he wrote some more in the dirt.

Hearing that, they walked away, one after another, beginning with the oldest. The woman was left alone. Jesus stood up and spoke to her. "Woman, where are they? Does no one condemn you?"

"No one, Master."

"Neither do I," said Jesus. "Go on your way. From now on, don't sin."[16]

Jesus has no stone to throw at you like others have. Dear friend, God is good. He loves you so much. He has great plans for you.[17] Plans greater than you can even imagine—beyond your biggest dream![18] Promises you can hardly believe, they are so wonderful. Like Cinderella's fairy godmother who made her attending the ball possible, only God's promises are no fairy tale and He is far greater than a fairy.

Dare you believe God's promises? Maybe someone gave you false promises in the dark. Maybe, like me, you kept looking for love in all the wrong places. The first guy who came along who paid you attention. The unavailable, married man. The jerk who treated you like crap. The drug addict you thought you could fix and save. The man who couldn't stop looking at porn, and expected you to look like the perfect, air-brushed models in the magazines. The controller who beat you, verbally and/or physically.

Or just the nice, stable guy who couldn't possibly fill up that universe-sized, black hole in your heart that only God could heal and fill. You thought a man was the answer to your problems. You kept running, searching like the Shulamite woman, desperately seeking for the one who would just love you for who you were, but kept getting hurt and coming up empty.

You believed those promises in the dark: "I love you." False expectations and desperate hopes for the love you've never had or known, in exchange for your body. You thought it was worth the price. You thought you had to give yourself to a man to be validated. You sold your soul to the devil, just to be held close and told you were beautiful.

> *All little girls should be told they are pretty, even if they aren't.*
> *~ Marilyn Monroe ~*

God thinks you are beautiful. You are being made into His masterpiece. God also whispers you promises in the dark, but His promises are the real thing:

> "So have no fear of them, for nothing is covered that will not be revealed, or hidden that will not be known. What I tell you in the dark, say in the light, and what you hear whispered, proclaim on the housetops." (Matthew 10:26-28, ESV)

> "I alone know the plans I have for you, plans to bring you prosperity and not disaster, plans to bring about the future you hope for." (Jeremiah 29:11, Good News Bible)

> "Be strong and courageous. Do not be afraid or terrified because of them, for the LORD your God goes with you; he will never leave you nor forsake you." (Deuteronomy 31:6)

"God can do anything, you know – far more than you could ever imagine or guess or request in your wildest dreams! He does it not by pushing us around but by working within us, His Spirit deeply and gently within us." (Ephesians 3:20, The Message)

You can count on God's promises. They are for real and they are forever.

PROMISES IN THE DARK

## Chapter 2
# abuse
# cinderella by the ashes

*"But whoever causes one of these little ones who believe in Me to stumble, it would be better for him to have a heavy millstone hung around his neck, and to be drowned in the depth of the sea."*
Matthew 18:6

My life has been like a nightmare, messy and filled with great pain. It all started with a family member having sex with me when I was just a child. But that doesn't sound very nice, does it? Maybe you can't relate. Maybe you had parents who loved you and grew up in a normal household—whatever "normal" really is.

Did you have an idyllic childhood—one filled with happy memories, flying kites, eating ice cream cones, riding bikes, enjoying picnics with your family? I had all of that, but there was a dark side to my life, too, a secret life that no one knew about.

I was sexually and physically abused in childhood, in horrendous ways. I worked through processing these terrifying memories in Christian counseling for five years to begin healing. God has done amazing, miraculous healing in my life, but I believe the healing will continue to be a life-long process.

My childhood sexual abuse by a male family member, as well as by other adults, lasted from early childhood until preteen years. I was physically abused until I left home and married at age seventeen.

To this day, as punishment for me confronting my family for the abuse, I was told that I was just crazy and am still being shunned by my family as if I don't exist, other than from my sister Maria, who is one of my best friends.

I was a pretty, quiet, painfully shy child with hazel-green eyes, an Irish round nose and a mouth with perfectly straight, pearl-white teeth. I had long, thick, chestnut-brown hair, and was short and petite. Introspective, a dreamer, I was creative and a writer; everyone else in my family was analytical, left-brained business people. My parents often received comments from friends and business peers on how beautiful I was.

As a baby, I weighed a little over six pounds. My mother told me later that the first time daddy ever saw me and held my tiny body in his arms, his heart was captured.

I love music. As a toddler, I'd beg daddy to play the guitar and he'd sing *My Only Sunshine*[19] to me again and again:

> You are my sunshine, my only sunshine,
> You make me happy when skies are grey.
> You'll never know, dear, how much I love you,
> So please don't take my sunshine away.

Mama often told me with an edge to her voice that I was daddy's "pet," always getting special treatment from him. When we would go to Dairy Queen on Friday nights as a family, everyone would order a vanilla or chocolate ice cream cone. But I'd ask daddy for a banana split and he'd buy me one.

One of my favorite meals was grilled, medium-rare steak with buttered baked potatoes or fried catfish with cheese grits and hushpuppies, and daddy would fix these sometimes as a special treat for me. (Oh, how I miss the fish fries since moving to the mid-west!) But I was never close to mama. My mother seemed to be jealous of me, especially as I entered the teen years, and I felt she hated me, sometimes verbally abusing me. I got into trouble with her much more frequently than my three siblings. She disciplined my older brother for talking back to her, but it was me whom she seemed to target. If I expressed anger of any degree, she said I was being "rude" to her and got out the belt to beat me.

As a result, I learned to stuff my anger deep inside until it festered into rage and became explosive anger in later years. My younger sister Maria and my younger brother, who we affectionately called "Bubba," seemed to get along well with her. They rarely got the belt. Maria seemed to be mama's favorite child. She has a different perspective of mama than I do, but today acknowledges that mama seemed to be much harsher in her treatment of me than the other siblings.

Mama often physically beat me with one of daddy's belts, leaving big purplish bruises on my thighs and lower back. His thicker, wider belt left bigger bruises, but the thinner belt was razor-sharp and its sting hurt worse, cutting deeper into my white skin.

I never felt really loved by mama, and don't understand why she seemed to hate me. Like Cinderella by the ashes, I never felt the warmth of love from her. Mama died when I was 18 years old, pregnant with my first daughter Heather. At her funeral, I mourned not for her, but for not being loved by her, for the mother I never had. God has been so good to bring spiritual mothers/mentors into my life to be the salve and balm on that deep wound, women who have loved, prayed for, and believed in me.

I'm thankful for the female friendships in my "real" life and my virtual ones online. I don't know what I'd do without these wonderful women of God. You know who you are! Speaker/author Jo Ann Fore concurs:

> Now I'm a big fan of social media. Love it. I have a ton of online friends, and I love them. God has connected me with absolutely amazing women online-beautiful women I may never have met otherwise. But for us, the deeper relationship comes when my friends and I intentionally pull offline, when we set a date for a hands-on, real-time connection. There is nothing that replaces the open-hearted power of a live, intimate conversation with a trusted friend.[20]

The only thing I could count on from my mother was her anger at me. Looking back on my childhood now, I recall my mother's eyes as slits of rage and hate, and believe my mother may have been mentally ill and/or oppressed spiritually. I believe it was Satan operating through her. It was really him who hated me so much. He was trying to hinder or stop my purpose and high calling from God. He has tried to hurt me and take my life many times since childhood.

Yet, "You intended to harm me, but God intended it for good to accomplish what is now being done, the saving of many lives."[21] In the last several years, God has used me many times when speaking and writing to minister to women who were physically and sexually abused in childhood. He has given me beauty for ashes.[22] Like Cinderella who had to sleep by fireplace ashes to stay warm and then became the Prince's chosen bride after she danced with him at the ball in her glass slippers, Jesus my Prince has transformed my life. This is the topic of my signature talk, *The Power of Shoes*.[23]

My childhood was lonely and unhappy, and fear cloaked me. I learned early on to keep the secrets of my childhood. In gym class at junior high school, we had to undress in front of each other and put on ugly, striped squash-yellow and white uniforms. One time my two friends saw the purple bruises on the back of my thighs and lower back, gasped, and asked what happened. I lied about it and then began hiding to undress for gym class, feeling ashamed and scared to tell the truth. Somehow I felt afraid that I was the one who would get into trouble (with officials and my parents), if anyone found out.

One time I gathered the courage to tell a school counselor that I was being abused at home. She said, "Beth, I know your family. You know that just isn't true."

My voice was silenced more that day.

> *Our souls stained, our hearts wrecked, we tend to lose hope. Our mouths broken, we fall silent. While silence can be serene and comforting when we need a break from daily living, silencing who we are, our internal voices, weakens our ability to connect heart-to-heart with others. Over time, our voices can fade to insignificance. The nothingness permeates our lives with low self-esteem and threatens to steal our very identities.*
> *~ Jo Ann Fore ~*
> *When A Woman Finds Her Voice*

Voiceless. Screaming inside for help but unheard, unseen by any. *Did I matter?*

If this happened today, she'd be required by law to report the abuse. That is the only time I recall ever telling anyone about my childhood abuse when I was growing up. I often wonder why nobody ever noticed anything going on, and why I wasn't rescued. I guess it was just well hidden. My parents had a good reputation as respected, successful professionals and were actively engaged in community services, so maybe nobody would ever suspect them of child abuse.

Yet anger was growing inside of me like a time bomb. I married very young to get away from home. While I hadn't had sex yet with my boyfriend, I often came home later than curfew, rebelling against my father's authority. One morning I mouthed off at daddy about his strict control over how often we could date, and he punched me, giving me a black eye. At school, I lied about this to friends, too, saying I had run into the door. If this occurred today, child protective services would be called and I would've been taken into protective custody.

One weekend when I violated curfew again, my dad forbade me to see my boyfriend for the entire week. He felt that we were "getting too serious too fast." Instead, I ran away from home with my boyfriend, causing my parents great distress.

My dad, my uncle, and my brother drove around town until late that night, searching in vain for us. We were at a friend's apartment, hiding from my father. I was too afraid to come home to face him.

Finally, my dad sat waiting on the back porch with a shotgun every night, intending to use it to shoot my boyfriend if he pulled up in the driveway in his souped-up Nova car. Just a heads up, any respectable Southerner has handguns, rifles, and shotguns to use as a warning for trespassers on their property…and sometimes for more than a warning, if the case warrants it.

> *My parents won't let me have a motorcycle, but they give me all the guns I want. I asked them for a motorcycle last Christmas and they told me I'd only kill myself. They got me this twelve-gauge instead.*
> *~ Scott Thompson ~*

Yeah, guns are a Southern thing—as well as protecting your family and land.

As a parent today, I can see why he would do something that seemed so crazy, especially regarding his child. Grief, fear, worry, and anger can cause you to react erratically sometimes. I get it. You can mess with me, but don't mess with my kids or grandkids; I'm like a mama tiger when it comes to protecting them. I realize today that my parents must have been beside themselves with worry over me when I ran away. They didn't know if I was dead or alive. I would've been in a panic if that were one of our daughters running away.

When I called home the second night, beginning to feel afraid of what my dad would do to us, I threatened to never come home again, unless they agreed to let me marry my boyfriend. To my shock, my dad called my bluff and agreed to give me legal permission to marry. I was still a senior in high school and not legally old enough in the state to marry. He realized with resignation that I was going to do what I wanted anyway.

In my father's mind, it was better to let me marry too young than for me to "shack up" with a boy, embarrass the family name and tarnish his business reputation. He didn't believe me that we hadn't had sex yet, but I hadn't. Back then, if you were "living together" with a man, you were considered "loose" (a whore/tramp).

After I ran away and daddy agreed for us to marry, I was too afraid of my father to stay at our family's house, so my paternal grandmother let me spend several nights with her before the wedding day. She spoke curtly to me, treating me coldly for the first time in my life. I think she believed I'd had sex, too. It hurt me, but I had worried everyone and the family was shunning me accordingly. This would be the first time I'd be shunned by them and it lasted just a few days; the second time has lasted over twenty years.

My father didn't believe our marriage would last, and he was right. Daddy seems to be a seer; many of his predictions about us four kids have come true.

We married in a small family wedding ceremony (in the wedding picture, my father looked like he could bite nails). My mother suggested that I wear that year's pretty, powder-blue prom dress as my wedding gown. She took me to a wedding shop to buy a white veil, and I looked longingly at the floor-length, elegant wedding dresses. Mama told my paternal grandmother this, and grandma said she'd buy me a beautiful wedding gown like I wanted. Her gift touched me deeply. I found one that I loved and it fit me like a glove. My mom gasped when she saw me in it; she said it was made just for me.

One of the attendees at the wedding later told me that when I turned the corner of the church to come down the aisle, the sun just then streamed through the stained glass windows, bathing me in a glorious light. He said it was as if God Himself was shining down upon me—His own Beautiful Bride.

> I will sing for joy in GOD,
>    explode in praise from deep in my soul!
> He dressed me up in a suit of salvation,
>    he outfitted me in a robe of righteousness,
> As a bridegroom who puts on a tuxedo
>    and a bride a jeweled tiara.
> For as the earth bursts with spring wildflowers,
>    and as a garden cascades with blossoms,
> So the Master, GOD, brings righteousness into full bloom
>    and puts praise on display before the nations.[24]

My mom threw together a pretty wedding for us in a matter of days. She made sure that we registered for fine china and silver for our wedding gifts. Years later, that china would become a big deal to my father during my first divorce; he made sure the papers included that the china had to be shipped to me from California (where we'd moved for my then-husband's truck driving job), as part of the divorce agreement since it was mama's idea in the first place for me to have fine china.

I think we only used it once or twice the whole time we were married. It's funny, during a divorce things like china become the larger issues to distract you from the thought of your marriage falling to pieces. We were only married one year, but the divorce took several years as my ex-husband procrastinated a long time filing the papers. What had gone wrong? Why wasn't it "happily ever after"?

> Most of the fights we've had as a couple have been over stupid things. And we're not alone. I was talking with one friend recently who told me that one of the first fights she and her husband had was about Dairy Queen. They'd been driving through Texas on their way to visit family and she'd mentioned she wanted to stop at the next DQ they passed. He kept driving. He doesn't love me anymore, she thought. These kinds of fights sound silly, but—for us anyway—it seems like the fights about little things are always the worst…
>
> Often we don't take these conflicts seriously because they're not really important. But the habits we use in these little disagreements set a pattern for how we react when big issues arise. That's why little arguments are a great place to start when it comes to building conflict resolution skills.[25]

A big issue did arise in Toben's and Joanne's marriage. She had a major stroke and is still recovering. Toben, her children, her parents, and her family have had to take care of her through the arduous journey. It was not something they were expecting:

> When I think of my stroke, I often think of it as a thief—something that stolen [sic] from me many of the things I care about—my home, my cat, my favorite clothes and shoes, running, dependence, my inability to do things like knit, crochet, hold open the pages of a book, the ability to take care of myself and my family, in many ways, I feel like having a stroke stole my life and gave nothing in return. The thought of living a long life has no appeal to me anymore, in many ways I already feel like an elderly person, dependents [sic] upon others for most of my needs.[26]

Yet Joanne continues to pray, relying upon God's faithful promises.

> I do not believe that I am living the kind of abundant life that God has promised me, the life that Jesus died to give to me. but [sic] I long to live and not just exist however, [sic] I am not sure how to go about living such an abundant life in my own power, and so all I can do is pray for such a life, to believe that God is who he says he is; he can do all he says he can do; he fulfills his promises, and that because those things are true, I can realistically hope for an abundant life in the land of the living.[27]

I've been praying for Joanne since I first heard online about her stroke and I'm standing in agreement in prayer with her for that abundant life for her. Her story has made my heart ache; I also praise God for the healing He has done in her life and will continue to pray for her complete healing (she still can't use her left arm/hand). She's an amazing writer (books and her blog); her writings are very transparent and filled with God's love and wisdom. I don't believe she realizes she offers abundant life to others through her writing. You can find her books for sale here: http://astore.amazon.com/thesimwifbyjo-20.

The abundant life is hard to achieve for most married couples. It's often the little foxes that spoil the vineyard.[28] My father wasn't surprised by my divorce, just aggravated by the expense of flying me and Heather home, taking me and the baby into his home to shelter us, paying for my vocational training to get on my feet, and dealing with my rebellion to his authority again.

He had been aggravated and angry at the wedding, an ice-cold stranger to me even as he walked me down the aisle. My boyfriend and I were married in a different church from the one my parents regularly attended; I guess they were too ashamed to use theirs and didn't want to answer any questions. They kept the guest list very small. Many people who did know wondered if I was pregnant, but I wasn't.

After we married, that same week mama was admitted into the hospital for heart problems. She already suffered numerous health problems and was on a slew of prescription drugs. I felt terribly guilty about her hospitalization, thinking my actions had caused this relapse. She was soon released, but her health continued to decline.

She and I got along better after I married and moved out of the house. I remember one time coming over after my college class was over. Her eyes lit up at the sight of me, one of the few times I recall her looking at me with any sort of affection.

"Hey," she said, smiling, "it's good to see you! Want a hot dog?" It is a Southern tradition to feed family and guests when they come over, a sign of hospitality. At that time, hot dogs were one of my favorite things to eat.

The last time I saw her, I'd come over to visit without calling first. My family seemed glad to see me as it had been awhile. I don't recall what mama and I talked about that day, but I'm glad that we'd been getting along better when she died. I chatted with my younger sister, then was going downstairs to leave for my apartment.

"Beth?" I heard my mother call from the den. Mama had a thick Southern accent, so when she said my name, it sounded like, "Bay-yeth." I felt a dart of guilt for leaving without telling her bye, and then said goodbye to her. That was my last time seeing her, and I'm thankful we parted on good terms.

That night, my mom asked my sister Maria to fix her a lettuce and tomato sandwich, and my sister got mad about it and argued with her, but did it anyway. To this day she carries guilt about this being their last conversation. Of course, she needs to forgive herself. But how important it is that we live each day as if it's our or others' last day. We're never guaranteed tomorrow.

> "Eventually, everything goes away."[29]

> "You were given life; it is your duty (and also your entitlement as a human being) to find something beautiful within life, no matter how slight."[30]

Mama's death was unexpected, despite her health problems. She was only forty-two years old. Months after my boyfriend and I married, when I was working at a convenience store early one morning, she died. All of the siblings but me were living at home.

She had fallen to the floor screaming about the unbearable pain in her leg. My father rushed to tell my older brother to call 911. My younger sister and younger brother were awakened from sleep at the commotion and were frightened, not knowing what was going on. My older brother later told me about the "smell of death" in the room when she died, which haunted me. The paramedics worked on her awhile when they arrived, but it was too late. She died in front of my father. Meanwhile, I knew nothing. No one had called me.

It was early and still dark outside. At the convenience store, I looked out the glass door and saw my then husband drive up to the store in his jeep, and knew something was wrong. It wasn't time for him to go to work yet. He came into the store crying.

"Bethy," he said (my mother's and his nickname for me), "I don't know how to tell you this, but your mother died this morning! Your family called to tell you!" I was in shock and called my boss, asking if I could leave to be with my family. He came to the store right away, relieving me from duty and gave me a week off work.

At the time, I was pregnant with Heather. I stayed at my parents' house for most of the day. My mom's cousin Gay took her kids, me and my siblings to the doughnut shop to comfort us. Southerners seem to answer every problem with food.

My mom's adoptive father had stock in Coke and someone had brought cases of glass bottles of Coke to the house. I drank them all day long, with my then husband harping at me about not needing to drink so many; he said it wasn't good for the baby.

My grandmother was on me about putting on a sweater, as I was wearing a maternity sundress with no bra, because the bra straps would show in back. But grandma felt it was indecent (it was!). It was May, already humid and hot, and I was very pregnant and already hormonal. There was no way I was putting on a hot, itchy sweater. I felt angry that all they cared about were Cokes and bras, when my mother was dead.

The doctor thought it was a blood clot in her leg, which traveled to her heart. I thought it was all the medications she was on, the prescriptions negatively interacting with each other. Years later, my father's girlfriend told me it was me who had killed my mother, for worrying her to death. I carried that false weight for years. I felt guilty enough that I'd caused my parents stress with my rebellion.

Prior to mama's death, my relationship with my parents and siblings had grown strained after the wedding. I rarely visited home. My father held his distance with me because I'd run away, which deeply hurt. I had become the "black sheep" of the family.

After I married, I went into major rebellion spiritually, experimenting with alcohol, drugs, and sexual immorality. It was like I just went wild. I felt guilty for what I was doing, and would tell God I was sorry for being "bad." I often didn't understand my own sinful behavior, and wondered why I was doing these things like getting drunk and having affairs. Much of my behavior was typical for sexual and physical abuse survivors; some therapists call it "acting out." Regardless of its cause, it was sin.

> So the trouble is not with the law, for it is spiritual and good. The trouble is with me, for I am all too human, a slave to sin. I don't really understand myself, for I want to do what is right but I don't do it. Instead, I do what I hate. But if I know that what I am doing is wrong, this shows that I agree that the law is good. So I am not the one doing wrong; it is sin living in me that does it...Who will free me from this life that is dominated by sin and death? Thank God! The answer is in Jesus Christ our Lord.[31]

The marriage was soon unhappy, filled with strife. The childish ideals of "fun" and "happily ever after" were quickly and surprisingly replaced with adult responsibilities like hard work, endless bills, college classes – and soon, taking care of a baby! I became pregnant a few months after being married, even though I was on birth control pills. But we were happy about the news.

My beautiful, precious daughter Heather was born out of that marriage which only lasted one year. After the divorce, I was a single mom for years, working and furthering my education at vocational training school and college, trying to stand on my own two feet and find my way to where I belonged.

Those were the "lost years" for me. Like a gypsy, I wandered from place to place, person to person, seeking, never finding, as described in the words of U2's song, *I Still Haven't Found What I'm Looking For*.[32]

I felt as if there were an enormous, black hole inside of me, a supermassive star collapsing in itself, and I was desperate to find something or someone to fill the hole before I too would collapse in myself and be no more. I recognize now it was a God-void. I was lonely and confused. I seemed drawn like a magnet to men who verbally and physically abused me, and who used me sexually— then threw me away. I didn't recognize my value and worth in Christ.

Later, I was married to a man who battered me and Heather physically and who was unfaithful. In my late 20s, we moved from the South where I'd been born and raised, to the mid-west for a "fresh start" (after discovering he'd had an affair with his ex-girlfriend), but I kept in contact with my family.

When he left the state and I divorced him, I suddenly began experiencing panic attacks, nightmares, frequent crying jags, and depression. Repressed memories of childhood abuse were suddenly surfacing, coming continually and obtrusively to the forefront of my mind, swooping at me relentlessly like a hawk after prey. I was being flooded with memories; the dam that held back early memories to keep my sanity intact was breaking and they rushed forward. I felt I'd drown from the fear.

> When you go through deep waters, I will be with you. When you go through rivers of difficulty, you will not drown. When you walk through the fire of oppression, you will not be burned up; the flames will not consume you.[33]

After I went to a hospital E.R. one weekend for an especially frightening panic attack that occurred while I was driving, the staff referred me to a therapist for follow-up outpatient help. This man turned out to be a divine appointment and godsend, a Christian counselor named Darrell.

For the next five years, I met with Darrell at least once a week for suicidal depression, panic attacks, anger, nightmares, and intense fears. As I began working in counseling, processing the childhood memories, overcoming cutting,[34] and coping with flashbacks and nightmares of sexual and physical abuse, I began getting breakthroughs in my healing. I was attending college, writing poems and in my journal, slowly making friends, spending time with Heather by taking long walks and feeding the ducks at the park, and learning that my past didn't have to define my future — but was bright with hope and faith in Christ.

Heather had short-term counseling, too, with a child therapist, to recover from her physical abuse from my second ex-husband and her sexual abuse from a babysitter's husband that lasted a few weeks. Never suspecting anything, I found out about this sexual abuse after Heather told me. I'd rushed in a fury to the babysitter's house to confront them, only for the babysitter's daughter to say that Heather and I were lying. The perpetrator's wife (the babysitter) believed us, however. The perpetrator had fled the country shortly before Heather told me and now we knew why. I reported it to the police, but little could be done since he had left the U.S. Heather progressed quickly in counseling, so her treatment time was much shorter than mine. It was vital to me that Heather grew up as "normal" as possible, with a better, happier life than I'd ever had.

By now I was in my late twenties and was tired of being alone, afraid, anxious, and depressed all the time. I was sick of the dating scene. I wanted a fulfilling Christian marriage, one that would last. I didn't like being unmarried or a single mom.

I was engaged to a man, but he'd been sexually abused in childhood, too, and we fed off each other's dysfunction. Our relationship began quickly deteriorating. I was hurting and lonely. One night I attended a Christian small group, which Darrell recommended that I visit to get support and to form friendships with other believers.

It was extremely cold outside that night and I was wrapped in a thick coat, hat and gloves. I took off my black gloves as our pastor's wife Vickie introduced me to Pat, one of Ray's closest friends, and Ray standing in the hallway. Pat was tall, lanky, with curly hair and glasses. I apologized for my cold hands as I shook his hand and he smiled at me, saying, "Cold hands, warm heart." I immediately loved him as a friend and knew we'd be friends for life as brother and sister in Christ.

Pat later married a beautiful Christian, Proverbs 31 woman named Kimberly, who today is one of my best friends. They have four beautiful and precious kids, Caleb, Nathaniel, Megan, and

Hadassah, who is their adopted Chinese girl. After marrying, Pat and Kim moved from Missouri to Pennsylvania to Jacksonville, Florida to be close to the beach. (Kim and I share a love for chocolate and the ocean!)

Although they are far away in distance, they are always close to our hearts. They are the type of friends who you can always pick right back up where you were talking, even if it's been months or years since you've seen each other.

Ray was shorter and stockier than Pat, with blonde hair and beautiful, deep blue eyes that reminded me of the ocean. I could tell right away looking into his eyes as we shook hands at the pastors' home that he was interested in me, which intrigued me. He held himself stiff and acted formally distant with me, that didn't fool me one bit and I thought was funny. Ray said that first night he met me, God spoke to him in his heart and said, "She's going to be your wife." He had heard right.

He invited me to his home group which he held each week in his home, where we got to know each other better. After six months of growing closer as best friends, we began dating.

Ray was a licensed minister who hosted a Bible study with 30 to 40 people in his home every Friday night, and he knew more about God and the Bible than anyone I'd ever met. I was like a sponge, absorbing everything I could from him, asking him question after question about the Bible until late in the night.

I was shocked to discover that the Bible had a book about romance and sex (Song of Solomon). Ray was amused and delighted to tell me about this book during our late night talks, because I had a distorted view about sex due to my childhood sexual abuse and my sexually immoral history. I thought sex was "bad." Ray shared from Song of Solomon with me, while trying to restrain his feelings and desires for me. He taught me about many other topics in the Bible, such as forgiveness, the baptism of the Holy Spirit, the spiritual gifts, and the sealing of the Holy Spirit at salvation (security of salvation).

I was beginning to learn about God's unconditional love and forgiveness, to heal with Ray's love and the love and acceptance of his friends in his home group. I'd never experienced this kind of love before, and what stood out to me was how much genuine joy they had—how much they laughed. Heather and I had fun going on Friday nights.

Ray had his own painful past to heal from and he was ready for a fresh new start. He wanted that fresh start with me. He was going through a painful divorce after his wife left him and their child to live with a man in another state; he was hurt and lonely. He gladly answered my questions after everyone left Bible study, having more than spiritual interest in me from the start, even though he knew I was engaged to another man. My mutual but guarded interest in him was balm to his rejected soul.

When my fiancé and I finally broke up (to Ray's glee), Ray and I were soon seriously involved in our relationship, with warnings from our church pastors to slow down. After asking his wife one last time to reconcile and she refused, he proceeded with filing for divorce. We called each other, talking late into the night. Each weekend I'd come over to his Bible study with Heather, and stay later than the other guests.

One night after several months of dating exclusively, he proposed on his front porch—sort of. "Marry me," he said, looking down at me in the light of the moon. "Okay," I answered. Not very romantic, but there it was.

We were blissfully engaged to be married, and we ignored the advice of our pastors and well-meaning friends to wait longer and not rush into marriage. I felt momentarily very happy; I was attending college classes, writing as a catharsis, and striving to be the best mom possible to Heather. She and I were glad that the worst days were over with my abusive ex-husband and all the wrong men I'd dated. Heather was very excited about our upcoming wedding, and so was Eden.

Ray's love gave me feelings of security and safety, emotional stability, and spiritual strength…the safety I needed for fully disclosing memories of the past, which I'd never told anyone. He asked me many questions about my past, knowing that shame thrives in darkness and that it would help heal me to confess what I'd done wrong with someone I trusted. I no longer had to hide like Eve with fig leaves. I could confess, repent and heal.

> Confess your sins to each other and pray for each other that you may be healed. The earnest prayer of a righteous person has great power and produces wonderful results.[35]

Ray also shared scriptures with me about forgiving all those who had hurt me. He shared unashamedly about his painful past, too. We were an open book with each other. We had similar interests and likes…but found out how very different we were *after* we married!

We talked for hours, about every topic under the sun. We enjoyed learning more about God, studying the Bible and worshipping together at home group. We also loved going out to eat dinner at different restaurants on dates, with him urging me to broaden my horizons by trying new types of food such as Japanese, Thai, and Greek. To this day, he still laughs at the memory of the Ouzo drink at a Greek restaurant that he bought me to "sample"; I couldn't walk when I got up from the table just from one drink. Ouzo is potent! The first and last time I ever drank it. Never again! Sometimes we went on dates alone and sometimes our kids went with us. We rode the roller coasters at Worlds of Fun, ate cotton candy, and just had a good, fun time. We went to movies and on long walks at the park and on nature trails. We wanted to bond as a family before marriage. My heart went out to Eden because her mommy had left, and she seemed to adore me. Ray and Heather loved each other from the start.

Ray had just gotten out of a fourteen-year stint in the Navy as a combat medic, was a licensed minister with his successful home church on Friday nights, and was applying for jobs as a paramedic. I planned to pursue a career in social work to become a therapist working with abused women—maybe I could find answers for my own vexed soul. I also wanted to become a best-selling author. Heather attended Catholic parochial school.

In planning our wedding and family life, we agreed that I'd take care of Eden during the daytime when Ray began working, when she wasn't spending time with her mother in another state. Oddly, the judge at the divorce hearing had ruled for a "month to month visitation" for little Eden—one month staying with Ray and me, the next visiting her mother for a month in a different state across the country.

This arrangement caused Eden years of stress and emotional instability (her mother married numerous times through the years, so she has had a lot of "stepdads"), but we had to comply since it was the judge's ruling in court. But we were excited about marrying and "becoming a family."

My therapist Darrell was happy for us, and thought our marriage would be a blessing to all of us for, "God places the lonely in families."[36] Darrell thought God would use Ray's love to help heal my brokenness and vice versa. (Ray, a child of divorce, had been verbally and physically abused in childhood as well, to a much lesser extent).

We discovered after marriage how hard it was. Ray's love would not be enough to heal me...or my respect to heal him. When victims marry, it gets messy. Marriage is challenging, but even harder when both parties are unhealed, bringing a lot of emotional baggage into the relationship. We brought a truckload of baggage! We didn't foresee these problems, though. We were just trying to think of how to afford to get married. Love would take care of it all, right? It was a wedding on a tight budget, but who cares as long as it's a pretty wedding with friends there, right?

A honeymoon? We'd do that later. (We actually did! For our tenth wedding anniversary, we flew to Switzerland, rented a car, and saw the breathtaking Swiss Alps, and drove to other countries like Italy, France, and Liechtenstein for ten days. It was wonderful, one of the happiest times of our marriage!).

For the wedding ceremony, I borrowed my friend Deanne's beautiful, floor-length, white-lace wedding dress that had a slight train, which fit me perfectly like a tee.

We'd picked up my bouquet of long-stemmed red roses with baby's breath (my favorite flowers besides white daisies and sunflowers) at the florist before going to the church to dress. The roses suddenly began turning black, and I began fearfully crying, "It's a SIGN!" My matron of honor, Deanne, and bridesmaid, Ellen, had to calm me down so I wouldn't back out of the wedding ceremony in an almost superstitious panic.

Ray rented a white tux and his grooms rented black tuxes. We asked the pastor of a church in our city, which we didn't even attend, to use the building during their Sunday morning worship time, to save money on renting a building. So we didn't know many of our wedding guests…but the room was full of guests!

A friend served as the photographer. Ray, always one to be different, hired a Scottish bagpiper to play *Amazing Grace*.[37] Ray's best man was Jim (Deanne's husband), and Ray's grooms were his other best friend, Pat, and Jim and Deanne's son Stephen, who accompanied Heather (my first bridesmaid) down the aisle.

Ellen also made the beautiful, elegant white wedding cake. At the reception after the wedding, she began wailing with big tears falling down her face that one of the cake's columns was sinking and the cake was ruined. She had worked so hard on it and wanted it to be beautiful for us. Was this another sign?

We had very few gifts from friends at the reception. A third sign? Our friends were just as poor as we were. But we had big dreams and new hopes in our heart…money didn't matter, right? Actually, money would turn out to be one of the biggest things we fought over for years!

For our honeymoon, Ray and I went back to my apartment, where we drank sparkling grape juice and I wanted to stay in the floor-length, white wedding gown for hours, sitting on the couch and talking to Ray. I felt beautiful in it and didn't want to take it off.

*The past would not be so easy to discard for us, either.*

Our girls were ecstatic. Ray's daughter Eden would get a new mother, or so she and Ray thought and hoped. She called her biological mother "Mommy Karla" and me "Mommy Beth."

Heather would gain not only a father, but a sister, too. At last, after such a long time waiting, Ray was my knight in shining armor…the one who'd rescue me and my child from the pain, the past, and the poverty. We'd live happily ever after, right?

Ray grew up reading and collecting comic and history books. Knights and comic book figures like Superman, Batman, and Superman were his heros. He had been working as a paramedic since he was nineteen years old, and was in the Navy for fifteen years, so he was a rescuer by nature. He thought he could rescue me, a lady in distress. He thought he'd be my superhero.

*Promises in the dark.*

For Heather, Ray was a gift from God—the loving and good father she'd always needed and longed for, who would love and protect her. Ray never made a difference in his feelings for or his treatment of any of our children. He loves Heather the same as his biological children, Eden and Leah (Leah is Ray's and my child together).

Heather's biological father never supported her financially and was not there for her physically or emotionally. To Heather, Ray is her father. She even had her last name legally changed to his name "Jones" before she married to show that she considers him her "real dad."

Ray is hers, Eden's, and Leah's big hero. He's the "fun dad." I'm the one who has made them eat their meals, drink water, brush their teeth, go to bed on time, and told them "no" about certain things—so I'm not nearly as fun as dad!

Heather's biological father didn't pay child support while she was growing up, so I struggled a lot financially as a single mom for many years. We didn't have much money, but I tried to think of fun, inexpensive activities we could enjoy together. We loved going for walks around the lake at the park and feeding the cute, quacking ducks crumbs of bread. This is one of my and Heather's happiest memories from her childhood.

When I married Ray, Heather enjoyed spending time with him as his "movie buddy," going for ice cream cones, and taking karate classes with him. Later, our whole family took karate classes under the fun training of our precious loving, funny friend Mike Fools, who is now passed away. Ray was trying to think of some activity to draw us together in unity and to keep us physically fit.

For me, adjusting to a blended family was much more difficult. It had just been Heather and me for years. I'm also a very independent person, so giving up my physical and emotional space was difficult. Ray had been diagnosed with Attention Deficit Hyperactivity Disorder as a child (ADHD)[38] and I suspected that Eden might have ADHD, too. Her incessant talking as a toddler from morning to late at night and her hyperactivity drove me crazy. It frustrated Ray too, but he was much more patient and understanding than I was. He did little about it, other than to tell me that I "just needed to love and accept her."

Ray's mom Judy told me once that while she dearly loved her son, Ray had talked nonstop and gotten into everything as a child, and it drove her wild. She often sent him outside to play to get out of her hair. Ray's dad had even less patience with him. I felt this way with Eden's behavior.

Eden's biological mother had left Ray and her for another man to live with in another state, and it confused Eden. She was very much a daddy's girl and adored him, but also loved and missed her mommy. When Eden was school age, her mom wanted primary custody of Eden. Ray was ordered to pay all legal fees during the divorce, and wanted to avoid a lengthy, expensive custody battle so he acquiesced. Eden lived with her mom up until her mid-teen years, when her mother sent her to live with us as she couldn't handle the misbehavior. Eden needed Ray's parental discipline, but he rarely disciplined her, which later turned out to be to Eden's detriment.

She was jealous of any attention I gave Ray and vice versa. She often tried to come between us, and stirred up strife between us. She told Ray many times that he just needed to divorce me because I was making him and her so unhappy. A collection of studies analyzed in Furstenberg's *Remarriage and Stepparenting* show that the child(ren) of divorce, in a custodial father's home, resent the stepmother and don't recognize her authority.[39] Like most children of divorce, she wanted her parents back together. I understood this but it hurt me.

I desperately wanted to be "a good mom" to her, but didn't know how.

My painful past of abuse had emotionally crippled me. I needed Ray just as much as she did, and I especially needed him to deal with Eden's rebellious behavior.

I felt nobody was hearing me, how overwhelmed I felt in trying to cope with her behavior. I cried many, many nights through the years from the stress of stepparenting and my difficult marriage. I felt so alone. Our family was hurting and dysfunctional. I didn't know how to fix it. I couldn't; only God could heal us as a family.

I wish I'd been a more loving, mature stepmom, but I didn't know how to deal with her behavior or the stress I was under. My stress level was going through the roof. I felt Ray was doing nothing to spiritually lead our family and to correct Eden's behavior. Where were the promises of God for our family? We lived in constant strife and turmoil.

I began praying for God to reveal the truth to Ray, his family, and his friends about Eden, because they all were blaming me for the problems and said I just needed to love her like a mature adult. What about someone loving me, especially Ray?

No one else was walking in my very difficult shoes, but they severely criticized me. I thought, let her go live with them and they'd see what I was dealing with! I loved her, I prayed for her, I was concerned about her, but I was battle-weary, overwhelmed from the stress, and I was tired of being judged by others who were just making assumptions about me, based on what Ray and Eden were saying about me. No one was talking with me to find out what I was going through or things from my perspective. They just thought I fit the role of "the wicked stepmother."

Ray was angry and bitter at me for the past and for not being the wife and the stepmother he thought I should be. When his family and friends told him he should divorce me and take Eden, he agreed, but didn't take action. He told others that I was the problem, although he acknowledged Eden had an attitude and was in rebellion.

The main things that caused us problems was Eden's attitude, habitual lying, the messes she made, and constant rudeness to me. She'd tell me that I wasn't her mom and she didn't have to obey what I said. This cut my heart deeply. Once again, Ray said the answer was "unconditional love." I told him that God's love includes discipline and correction; He disciplines those He loves.[40]

When I'd finally lose my temper with Eden, especially after Ray refused to deal with her misbehavior, she'd tell her teachers, friends,

Ray's family and Ray's friends about what a horrible stepmother (her "stepmonster") that I was. I was judged and ostracized, without anyone calling or meeting me to find out the truth.

During these years, I felt more alone than I'd ever felt in my entire life. I thought constantly about leaving Ray and Eden, taking Leah with me to the beach or somewhere else to live. I developed stress-induced hypertension and had to go on high blood pressure medication.

During those years that Eden lived with us, I went through one of the worst nightmares of my life. Leah suddenly began having grand mal seizures at night that seemed to be cyclical—about once a month. After the second one, her neurologist diagnosed her with epilepsy. I began developing insomnia, terrified each night that she'd have a seizure and could possibly die. I was especially afraid on nights when Ray was on overnight shifts at the fire station. My worst fear was that she would stop breathing or her heart would stop and I'd be unable to revive her by CPR. I didn't feel confident in my CPR skills and wanted Ray there with me.

This nightmare lasted for several years until Jesus miraculously healed her. He had given me a promise and many scriptures for Leah's healing when the seizures first started. Her neurologist, who I believe was sent by God into her life, actually prophesied this. He said he believed one day they would stop. Other people told me this, too. I had to stand on the promise, while God taught me to have strong faith in the trenches of spiritual warfare. Next to Heather's brain surgery, it is the worst thing I've ever gone through in my life.

During that time, God spoke to me that He was going to supernaturally heal Leah. He gave me Casting Crown's song *Voice of Truth*[41] to comfort me and strengthen my faith. I'd hear it on the radio as I was driving somewhere and tears would pour down my face. I'd listen to it again and again on my CD player for encouragement.

God sent several prophets into my life to prophesy Leah's miracle healing: my husband Ray and our daughters Heather and Eden; Pastor Jay Threadgill of Fishers of Men International of Port au Prince, Haiti; Pastor Eddie Mitchell of Montgomery, Alabama; Benny Hinn of Benny Hinn International; Julia Klinefelter of Harrisonville, Missouri; Blanch Hershberger of Harrisonville, Missouri; Diane Bishop of Harrisonville, Missouri; Debbie Campbell of Harrisonville, Missouri; Crystal Tinsley of Harrisonville, Missouri; Betty Spangler of Harrisonville, Missouri; Suzy Bunton of Peculiar, Missouri; Royce Wilson of Harrisonville, Missouri; and Frances Lawrence of Butler, Missouri. I had to hold onto these words for dear life during the storm to emotionally anchor me. I had never felt so emotionally fragile.

When Eden and I were having the greatest trouble, I was in fear about Leah's seizures, homeschooling Leah, concerned over my oldest daughter Heather's very troubled marriage, and Ray and I were facing severe financial problems and foreclosure of our home during the housing crisis. During this time, I battled fears about Leah's life, hopelessness about my marriage and our finances, and condemnation as a stepmother.

The stress I was under was definitely a factor in my problems with Eden, but not an excuse. I felt guilty for being such a "bad stepmom," and repented frequently for not showing her Christ-like love. But I felt angry that Ray or anyone wasn't helping me to deal with the enormous stress in my life or with Eden's wrong behavior. I cried constantly at night, praying, begging God to help me and give me an answer. Looking back, I realize now we should have sought professional family counseling.

I didn't have the emotional tools I needed to cope with Eden's acting-out behavior, which closely resembled my own from the past. In fact, we were a lot alike, and that is probably why we had so many problems getting along! We both wanted control, and we both wanted Ray to ourselves. She was a troubled young girl crying out for love and acceptance, and yes, Ray's discipline. I was overwhelmed from all the stress in my life, and was crying out for love, too.

Eden began applying for jobs and was fired from her first job for her attitude, and other jobs after that. She failed and dropped out of two Christian schools, even though she's highly intelligent. Children of divorced parents are roughly two times more likely to drop out of high school than their peers whose parents didn't divorce.[42]

God spoke to my heart to just be quiet and get out of the Holy Spirit's way. It was then that she started arguing with and rebelling to Ray's authority. He was beginning to see that her attitude and her mouth were part of the problem, not just me.

She and I butted heads and argued loudly constantly. She moved out of our house the week she and Ray had their biggest argument over her continual refusal to obey the dating curfew and her disrespectful attitude toward Ray. The light was coming on, and he was finally seeing how she'd been acting toward me for years.

She and her boyfriend were engaged and wanted to marry. We didn't want them living together unmarried, and we sat down and talked to them both about the seriousness of their decision and how hard marriage was going to be for them. They said they understood, so Ray gave his permission and even officiated as the minister at the wedding.

Eden's marriage at the age of eighteen only lasted a few years, and the father now has primary custody of their son Jacob. Eden has visitation rights on the weekends and during holidays. Since leaving home, Eden has gone through the school of hard knocks.

As a parent, it's hard to watch your child go through trials and difficulties. The natural inclination is to rescue them out of all their troubles, but sometimes that can cripple them emotionally. But sometimes the most loving thing to do is nothing but pray, so they can learn the lessons they need to.

There are times when your adult children will make decisions you don't agree with, such as Eden and Heather getting tattoos and living with a man before marriage; you raised them in the fear of God and they will choose another path. In those times, you hold onto God's promise in Proverbs 22:6. I like the Amplified Version for this verse, because every child is uniquely created by God and has his or her own distinct personality, spiritual gift(s), and person. No two children are alike, and you can't do the same cookie-cutter parenting with all your children, but treat them as individual persons:

> Train up a child in the way he should go [and in keeping with his individual gift or bent], and when he is old he will not depart from it.[43]

To her credit, today Eden is a beautiful woman, spiritually gifted, highly intelligent, generous, very creative and artistic, hilarious like Ray, outgoing, friendly, and sunny. She's very funny, warm, and makes friends easily. She's a good mom to her son Jacob, and is a good sister to Heather and Leah.

She's now trying to get her life together. I see spiritual growth in her the last several years. She's now living in Oregon with her mom to get back on her feet again, and her mom is going to help her buy a car, find a job (hopefully at a bakery, which she loves to do, making cupcakes), and save money. She's considering further education. Then she'll move back to the mid-west to be with our family and her friends.

I've had to repent to God and to Eden for not loving her unconditionally as God does, and for not being a good and godly stepparent to her. While we still struggle in our relationship, I do feel it's better now. It's been a long road for us all. It was so hard when we lived together when she was a teen.

It wasn't easy raising Heather, either. She went through a short period of rebellion in her teen years. She began failing some classes at school and hanging out with the wrong crowd, trying cigarettes and alcohol. We quickly acted to squash this rebellion, becoming stricter with her activities with friends and dating curfews. Our family and friends severely criticized us, saying we were too strict, but I believe our fast intervention saved Heather's life. She was at a critical crossroad.

God spoke to my heart to begin homeschooling her at the end of her tenth-grade year. As our homeschool journey developed, God spoke to Heather's heart to become a missionary. She graduated from our homeschool, attended and graduated from Youth With a Mission (YWAM) missionary training school, and went on missions trips to South America and India for a month each. She also did stateside missions trips. Her goal and dream was to be a missionary in a foreign land.

After her YWAM graduation, she moved back home and was preparing to go to the mission field, but soon moved out to marry her first serious boyfriend. I believe the main reason she did this was because of our marital strife. It drove her away. Shortly after marrying, she became pregnant (twice). They gave us our two beautiful granddaughters, Annabelle and Violet.

Unfortunately, Heather's own marriage ended after ten years when her husband suddenly moved out and announced he no longer believed in God and was an atheist. Their marriage, as well as Eden's, was marked by strife. Children learn what is modeled. The Bible also says that the sins of the father visit to the third and fourth generation.[44] Both our daughters, sadly, were children of divorce and became a divorce statistic, something we never wanted to happen to them.

Today Heather is a single mom. She works for a chiropractor's office as his front desk receptionist, attends college time for a degree in business management, and runs 5K races. She has primary residential custody of their children. She went through a lot of pain and financial struggles after her divorce. I believe a single mom is the hardest job in the whole world. Other than my brief second marriage, I was a single mom for nearly a decade. The weight of the responsibilities falls mainly on the mother's shoulders in a divorce. The stress, especially financial, is intense. If the kids get sick, as all children do with colds, viruses, sore throats, etc., she's the one who has to take off work to take care of them and go to the doctor—which then affects finances. It's been so hard for me to watch her and Eden go through this suffering as single moms.

I think Ray believes that maybe he was too strict with Heather, so he went overboard with Eden, being much too lax in disciplining her.

I deeply regret not being more patient, kind and understanding with Eden. I acted immature with her. I desperately wanted to love her as my own children, but just didn't know how. I tried to not make a difference like Ray didn't, but there was a difference. My own children didn't treat me the way she did and didn't want Ray's and my marriage to be destroyed.

It hurt that she talked about me to everyone, painting me in the worst possible light at her "wicked stepmother" and even outright lying about me.

She often told Ray to divorce me. Looking back over it, I see why she felt that way. I failed miserably as a mom to her. I didn't love her the way she needed. I showed partiality between her and my children.

I felt inadequate for the job. I just kept praying, many times with tears pouring down my face because I felt so alone and so judged and misunderstood about my relationship with Eden.

One time at church, a prophet of God visited and I asked him for prayer. Without telling him a word about my situation, by the Spirit of God, he began to prophesy into my life concerning Eden, saying that God was going to do a new thing with the relationship and heal our very troubled parent-child relationship. I've held onto that promise for years, as well as God's promise to me that He will one day heal and restore my marriage.

> See, I will do a new thing. It will begin happening now.
> Will you not know about it? I will even make a road in the wilderness, and rivers in the desert.[45]

Eden's and my relationship today is much improved, but has a long way to go. We've always had a hard time getting along. I often pray for God to help me love her with His agape love. She calls me "mom" today and we tell each other we love one another, but I hope one day we will have a closer relationship.

On her Facebook wall, Eden recently posted a picture that says, "Stepparent: A stepparent is a truly amazing person. They've made a choice to love another person's child as their own."

Above the picture, she posted: (I have corrected her spelling errors here, but otherwise, this is exactly what she wrote):

> Beth Jones and Terry Austin, although I don't consider them "step." They are my real parents. My mom Beth and I have not always seen eye-to-eye and at some times we'd go head-to-head. For 23 years she's cared for me, prayed for me and that is why she is my mom. Terry took me in from the moment we locked eyes; even with him and my mom being divorced, he's still stuck by and I'm truly blessed for that. I'm so blessed to have two dads and two moms. It's an abundance of love that I'm so grateful for.

This truly blessed me.

When Ray and I first married, I was depleted emotionally working through childhood abuse memories and felt I didn't have the psychological resources to cope effectively with Eden's non-stop talking and hyperactive, erratic behavior. I was already in crisis with my family of origin and with my marriage to Ray.

Just before Ray and I married, I was working hard in counseling and thought I was ready to deal with my family about my childhood abuse through a confrontation. I wanted to let the past go and step into a brighter and happier future.

To move forward, I had to forgive. This is something that is so hard, but is essential to Christian growth. Forgiveness is a big key to healing from pain in your past. Unforgiveness, which can grow into the ugly sins of resentment, revenge, and bitterness, keeps you the prisoner.

I knew as a Christian I had to forgive my perpetrators and my family, because God commands it in His word—no matter what they had done and even if they never apologized, admitted what they'd done, or asked my forgiveness.

> But if you refuse to forgive others, your Father will not forgive your sins.[46]

I also knew that in order to marry Ray, I couldn't carry the baggage of the past into our marriage. I know for our marriage to heal today, I have to forgive my family, his, Eden, and others. Forgiveness sets you the prisoner free.

God's promises are not always happy, make-you-feel-good, rainbow-colored ones. They can also be warnings of dark, dire judgment if we disobey His word. God is holy and we as His people are to be holy, too.

If you and I are Christians, God has forgiven us of our sins, once and for all, and completely. He doesn't keep reminding us of our sins. Jesus paid for our sins at the cross to redeem us and our sins are washed white as snow.[47] God removes our sins as far as the east is from the west.[48]

So forgiving others is not an option…no matter how much they have hurt us. Forgiving doesn't mean we allow further abuse or mistreatment from others. But forgiveness allows you to walk in freedom, joy and peace, unshackled to the past.

I don't think that forgiveness means that we'll forget what happened. I do know, from my own experience, that the "sting" of the emotional pain lessens over time and you will think about the hurt less and less as the years go by and you become healthier. God's healing is deep and thorough. When you are focused on and enjoying the present, living your life fully and walking in your purpose, you won't need to keep looking in the rear view mirror.

Live today in this moment! Really live and be filled with gratitude to God for each and every day and all your blessings. Cultivate thankfulness for all God's done and will do! He's worthy of our worship and praise! If you'd like a great book on cultivating gratitude in your life, consider *One Thousand Gifts* by Ann VosKamp.[49]

I haven't forgotten the past, but I'm no longer in bondage to it. My past doesn't define me; God defines me. My value and my worth are in Him, not in what's happened to me or what I have done in the past.

My strongest spiritual gifts are prophecy, discernment, giving, and teaching, which I use through speaking, writing, and other forms of communicating. (For further study of the spiritual gifts, see Romans 12:6-8, 1 Corinthians 12:7-11, and Ephesians 4:11.)

A person who is spiritually gifted by God in prophecy and teaching is compelled to seek and to reveal the truth to themselves and to others—God's biblical truth. There is little to no grey area for those with these gifts! Things are either black or white!

So I felt that I needed a direct confrontation with my family, too, to move forward. I just wanted them to admit that it happened and then I would say that I'd forgiven them of everything. Just tell the truth! Simple and easy, right? It would be the first time I ever confronted them with the abuse.

When I flew home over twenty-three years ago and confronted my perpetrator, he said it wasn't true and told me and the family I was crazy. They believed him. Other than my younger sister Maria who believes me, my family of origin denies my childhood abuse. My family stopped speaking to me after that and made no more effort to contact me by phone, letter, or visits.

Like the Amish practice of shunning members who have "transgressed" and must be purged from the church and community[50], my family shunned me for over twenty years, not speaking to me because I had "alleged" abuse.

When I moved to the mid-west, one family member flew out once a year to visit me and my daughter, but stopped visiting us after my confrontation and no longer spoke to me. He still has nothing to do with me to this day, despite my efforts at writing him, sending Christmas and birthday gifts, and sending encouraging messages on Facebook. For over twenty years, my family acted as if I had never existed or had been born. Any time my name was brought up by my sister Maria, the peacemaker in our family, the subject would be changed.

I carried this wound into my marriage with Ray. I battle feelings of rejection each day from the way my family treats me, but I know that God loves me and cherishes me. My value is in Him and what Christ did for me, not what others think of me. I choose to accept God's love rather than my family's rejection.

Denial and shunning aren't an unusual experience for abuse survivors. As I shared in my book *The Hands Of A Woman: Everyday Women In Everyday Battles*[51], many sexual abuse victims are told by perpetrators to keep it a secret, and when they finally disclose it to their family members, they are called crazy, liars, or troublemakers, and are told to forget about it.[52]

Writer Vicki Messer experienced the same thing when she finally got the courage at age fifty-one to share the secret she'd been carrying her whole life about her childhood sexual abuse. The abuser had been dead eleven years.[53]

It sent shock waves through the family, and she was blamed instead. She had become the enemy. Her feelings and thoughts, her pain, were less important than maintaining the dignity and the "honor" of the now deceased abuser.[54]

The denial of the family inflicts even more damage, especially shame, on the victim.[55] Some family members die in their denial, which is sad. The truth is what sets people free, but some people never find that freedom in life.

What do you do when your family stops being your family? Your family represents your very identity and *the* source of unconditional love. When that identity is stripped from you, who are you? If your own family won't love and accept you, who will? God. He won't ever turn His back on you. He will never stop loving you, no matter what others do and no matter what you do. God has many beautiful promises in the Bible about this.

> Even if my father and mother abandon me, the LORD will hold me close. (Psalm 27:10, NLT)

> The eternal God is your refuge, and underneath are the everlasting arms. (Deuteronomy 33:27, NIV)

Your true identity is through your relationship with Jesus Christ. Your very existence is through and because of Him.

> For in Him we live and move and have our being. (Acts 17:28, NIV)

Your identity is "child of God"—son or daughter of God.

And I will be your Father, and you will be my sons and
daughters, says the LORD Almighty. (2 Corinthians 6:18, NIV)

We can take comfort in these passages. But it still hurts deeply when your family turns away from you.

**The Effects of Shunning**

A great movie about being ostracized by your family for your actions is *The Shunning*. It's about a girl who is shunned by her Amish family for singing songs that are other than hymns and for playing the guitar.

As it turned out, she wasn't actually Amish (her biological birth mother had given her away to the Amish family). In the end, her family reconnects with her emotionally. This is rarely done among the Amish.

The Amish are not the only group of people who practice shunning.

Some ultra-orthodox Jewish congregations hold funerals for former members who decide to marry outside the religion.[56]

You can see a clear example of this line of thinking in the movie, *Fiddler on the Roof*[57], when the papa Tevye says his daughter Chava is now dead to him after she eloped with the Gentile man, Fyedka. Tevye would no longer speak to his daughter, even when she was standing right in front of him. He acted as if she was invisible and wasn't there, despite Chava's heart-breaking cries and pleading to him.

When my family stopped speaking to me, *I felt invisible and insignificant, like I did not matter.*

Shunning is a form of punishment. Scientologists also practice shunning called "disconnection," which forbids its members from interacting with a "suppressive" person who leaves the religion. This includes no calls, no letters, and no contact.[58]

When Tom Cruise's wife, Katie, left him, taking their daughter Suri, Scientology's defectors spoke out, saying the church was bending rules and that Katie and Suri should have been labeled a "Suppressive Person"—shunned and cut off from all relationships.[59]

Shunning is also practiced by Jehovah's Witnesses. When a Jehovah Witness is "disfellowshipped," all members including immediate family must stop any contact. His or her status has changed, and he or she is no longer welcome in the home.[60]

In some cultures and religions, violators of doctrine can be put to death.

Emotionally, shunning is like death. Its effects on the "shunned" person are profound, such as causing feelings of rejection, loneliness, isolation, depression, discouragement, shame, false guilt, stress, fear, anger, and hopelessness.

Do any of these feelings sound like something God would want you to feel? No.

## Shunning is Like the Treatment of Lepers

We see an example of shunning in the Bible with stories about lepers. In Jesus' day, lepers were ostracized and confined outside the city limits, many times to the city dump.[61] They were considered outcasts in society. Anyone with leprosy had to shout, "Unclean! Unclean!" if anyone approached near him or her, as a warning.

Leprosy was repulsive and was incurable by human means, and thus feared by people. It was considered the physical counterpart to the spiritual problem of sin.[62] That's why it was called a "cleansing" instead of a "healing" when you were healed of leprosy. If you touched someone with leprosy, you were considered ceremonially unclean.[63]

Yet look at Jesus' response to a leper in Mark 1:40-45:

> A man with leprosy came and knelt in front of Jesus, begging to be healed. "If you are willing, you can heal me and make me clean," he said.
>
> Moved with compassion, Jesus reached out and touched him. "I am willing," he said. "Be healed!" Instantly the leprosy disappeared, and the man was healed. Then Jesus sent him on his way with a stern warning: "Don't tell anyone about this. Instead, go to the priest and let him examine you. Take along the offering required in the law of Moses for those who have been healed of leprosy. This will be a public testimony that you have been cleansed."
>
> But the man went and spread the word, proclaiming to everyone what had happened. As a result, large crowds soon surrounded Jesus, and he couldn't publicly enter a town anywhere. He had to stay out in the secluded places, but people from everywhere kept coming to him.[64]

Jesus, the Son of God, the Messiah, the Holy One, He of all people should have shunned this man. But He didn't. He loved him and had compassion on him. He went even further, doing the unthinkable in that society—He reached out and *touched* him. Remember, anyone who touched a leper would be considered ceremonially unclean by the Jews. But those were man-made laws. God's law of Divine, unconditional love is higher than man's law.

The Bible doesn't say this man sinned and the leprosy was his fault.

The Jews made the *assumption* that leprosy instantly meant the person was in sin and that it was the physical evidence of sin. They judged by outward appearance, not the heart. Today we would know that leprosy is Hansen's disease, caused by bacteria. It is now effectively treated and curable if diagnosed early.

The point of the passage is that God wants to show us the appropriate response to lepers and others with disease or emotional wounds.

> References to leprosy have a different emphasis in the New Testament. They stress God's desire to heal. Jesus freely touched people with leprosy.
>
> While people with leprosy traditionally suffered banishment from family and neighbors, Jesus broke from the tradition. He treated lepers with compassion, touching and healing them.[65]

## We are All Lepers, Who Need to be Touched by Jesus

My family's response to my confrontation about my childhood abuse was highly inappropriate and exposes the family's dysfunction. Like a leper, I had been defiled and contaminated by sexual and physical abuse. I was wounded and needed healing. My family's response should have been acknowledgment of the truth, a request for my forgiveness, and an apology for causing me such incredible physical, spiritual, and emotional pain — and an effort at reconciliation. That didn't happen. My family's dysfunction — the sexual and physical abuse, the alcoholism, the denial — was like leprosy, too.

My family never admitted what happened to me. They just wrote me off as "crazy." Instead of them apologizing and asking forgiveness, God dealt with my heart. With His still, small voice, He spoke to me and said that as a Christian, I had the ministry of reconciliation within me. (2 Corinthians 5:19)

I needed to be the mature one to reach out to them. They, too, were lepers and needed touching and cleansing. We, as human beings born with the Adamic sin nature, are all lepers who need Jesus' touch. I needed to model Christ's forgiveness to my family, since they didn't even know Him (forgiving them, without allowing them to further abuse me). My healing and cleansing would have to come from Jesus, not my family. And theirs, too.

> Now all things are of God, who has reconciled us to Himself through Jesus Christ, and **has given us the ministry of reconciliation**, that is, that God was in Christ reconciling the world to Himself, not imputing their trespasses to them, and has committed to us the word of reconciliation.[66]

Several years ago, I flew to Georgia and extended God's agape love to my family members. I told them I loved them. I talked with them and let them know that I didn't harbor any unforgiveness in my heart toward them. I had forgiven and let the past go. I wanted to move forward. I had broken the over twenty-year, cold silence between us by reaching out first.

They made an effort to restore their relationship with me, although admittedly there was still some distrust on both sides. Not all of them sincerely reconciled with me, though, and just made a good appearance of it. One family member, who hugged me when he saw me and told me he loved me, still continues to act as if I don't exist, which is extremely painful to me. It's as if I am invisible or was never born.

His behavior makes me feel *unloved and like I do not matter*. Just what Satan wants me to feel and believe. Ultimately, Satan is trying to abort my purpose and my calling from God, using my family's rejection as the tool to cause me to not believe God loves me, and to doubt my significance and identity in Christ.

Because I refuse to retract what I said about my childhood abuse (how can I deny the truth?), this family member won't forgive me... and he is not even the perpetrator, who does speak to me now! But I have done my part and when I go before God's judgment seat, I know I have obeyed Him. I did what God said. I forgave and showed my family Christ's love. Their response to me is between them and God.

**You Can't Pick Your Relatives!**

Maybe you've heard the old saying, "You can choose your friends, but you can't choose your family." Wouldn't it be nice if we could? While it would be ideal to live in a perfect family who shows you perfect, unconditional love, the truth is that all families have problems.

Some of those issues may be:

- Marital strife
- Struggles with rebellious children
- Health issues
- Financial hardships
- Bankruptcy
- Home foreclosure
- Work or ministry crises
- Domestic violence
- Car accidents or other tragedies
- Child abuse and/or neglect
- Alcohol, drug, gambling and/or pornography addiction
- Separation and/or divorce

God didn't promise us when we became Christians that life would always be easy. In fact, after you get saved, that's often when the battle intensifies. Satan hates you because you are a born-again, Spirit-filled believer. If he can't kill you, then he will do everything he can to keep you from accomplishing your God-given, great calling and mission.

> The thief's purpose is to steal and kill and destroy. My purpose is to give them a rich and satisfying life.[67]

The good news is that Jesus is greater than Satan. He wants to bless you and give you an abundant life through Him. Yes, dear friend, life will be hard at times. The Bible tells us that as believers, we will go through trials and tribulations, even with our family members. (I think *especially* with our family!) Yet Jesus came to give you peace and strength to victoriously endure any trouble.

> But take heart, because I have overcome the world.[68]

Your trouble may be family members or others who are shunning, rejecting or hurting you in some way. Maybe you, too, have experienced childhood sexual, verbal, or physical abuse. Maybe a parent is still trying to abuse you, or a spouse, a child, or a friend. Sheryl Griffin writes in her book, *A Scarlet Cord of Hope*, that she had to set clear boundaries with her alcoholic mother, who abused her:

> I do not know if my mother has sought treatment or if she is just careful not to call anymore when she is drunk. If she has sought any kind of treatment she has not shared that with me. The boundaries I have in place have helped me to have less anxiety and worry about my mom. I cannot deal with her until she deals with her addictions and emotional issues. Both of these issues, I believe, run deep within her. I do love

my mom. I do hope and pray for her daily. I know that God is in control and I have not given up on her, but I cannot give her the help she needs. I cannot save her. She needs to make those choices herself.[69]

Maybe you have been treated abusively or shamefully like a leper by your family or others. I urge you to forgive those who hurt you, and most of all, to reach out for Jesus to touch you. He is willing to miraculously heal and cleanse you of your pain.

When He does, be sure to thank Him. Then show others that same compassionate love and mercy—even those who have hurt you. You may have to set strict boundaries in your relationship with them, as Sheryl did. God can turn things around 180 degrees for you. He will use what was meant for harm for good for His glory, as He did Joseph, prince of Egypt.[70]

**Abuse Messed Me Up Badly!**

Just this morning, my husband Ray was talking about how my childhood abuse had caused me severe mental issues. The abuse messed me up bad. It has affected my entire life—every area of my life.

My inability to relate properly to people. My marriage to Ray especially (it's been hell!). My parenting—I've always been an overprotective, anxious mom, terrified something bad would happen to my children. My thought processes, like a dark, twisting, fearful, angry matrix. My turbulent, wild emotions. Lack of job/career stability. My focus crippled in school and college. My doubts about my speaking and writing. My sense of worth and value destroyed. My purpose and calling questioned intensely.

All abuse survivors ask, "Why?" I've asked it, too. I've never found an answer to it.

I don't know why my family won't really love me and still punishes me by not speaking to me. I don't know why I was abused. I don't know why God allowed it. I truly believe that God didn't cause the abuse; Satan is the one who did this to me (and to all abused people). The Bible says he is the thief who kills, steals and destroys.[71]

Yes, God is omnipotent, sovereign and could have stopped my abuse. God knew about it and *allowed* it. I don't know why He did. The truth is that bad things happen to good people. Bad things happen to the innocent, even children and babies.

God created everything, including man and woman, and said it was very good.[72] When Adam and Eve were deceived by Satan and sinned in the Garden of Eden, it opened the door for evil and chaos to destroy humans' lives.[73] We live in an unpredictable, scary world, where sin rages like a red-eyed beast and the consequences are life altering. Our souls scream. Like the scream of a mother whose child's life was suddenly snatched away.

Currently I'm coaching a client (Vickie) whose teen daughter, Hope, was tragically killed in a car wreck several years ago. A teen girl, who didn't have her license yet, took her father's keys, and went with a car full of friends into town. She was driving too fast, lost control, and her vehicle struck Hope's car head-on. My client's daughter had other teens in the car with her that night and had dropped them off at home. They were still alive and well. The teen driver whose car hit hers and her friends lived, too.

"All the teens in those cars went home, but my daughter, who went to the funeral home that night," Vickie said, and her words gripped my heart. I ached for her. We question why these things happen. Why did she die? Why did everyone else live but her?

"Beth, I have to believe that God is in control. And that it was her time to die," my client said. She still grieves, although God is continuing to heal her broken heart.

I have to believe, too, that God is in control and for whatever reason; He allowed my abuse, even though He didn't want this to happen.

I believe it broke His heart and He cried over me as I was being abused, just as Jesus wept over Jerusalem.[74]

Sometimes I wonder how different my life would've been and would be like now if I hadn't been abused as a child. What kind of woman would I be today? Would I have had a happier, more fulfilled life? Would I have lived a purer (less sinful) life? Would I be a more wonderful, godly wife and mom? Would I be a better, less self-absorbed friend? Would I have achieved more success in my business?

Surely I wouldn't have left home and married while still in high school. Or married my second husband. Or had all the relationships with men that I had, trying to find love in all the wrong places. And because I wouldn't have had all those relationships, maybe I wouldn't have gotten pregnant out of wedlock three times and had three abortions (or any).

I can't blame my family or my abuse for my sinful choices, but possibly I would've made different, wiser choices if I wasn't so screwed up in the first place.

I believe with all my heart that if I hadn't been abused, my marriage to Ray would've been totally different. He and I both would've been spared much of the pain we've gone through. Not all of it, but a lot of it.

Ray hasn't been able to heal me, no matter how hard he's tried. His patient, taxing efforts for over twenty-two years to convince me of his love, sometimes to the point of his emotional and spiritual exhaustion, haven't been enough to mend my shattered soul. Only God and His agape love and consuming power can heal me.

> This love is the greatest of all virtues; it is transforming; it is powerful; it never fails.[75]

Sometimes I look at people who had good, happy childhoods and I envy them. Parents who loved and hugged them. Parents who taught them about Jesus.

Parents who would never strike them on the back of the thighs and back with a razor-sharp belt or a thorny switch from a bush or call them bad names.

Parents who encouraged them that God had great plans for their lives. A family where little girls are never molested and filled with shame and self-loathing. And threatened to be quiet about it, or else.

After Maya Angelou was raped by her mother's boyfriend at eight years old, her mother realized her being in bed, acting lethargic, and saying she wasn't hungry was more than measles and took her to the hospital.

After she told her brother Bailey what happened, the nurses told Maya that now there was nothing more to fear and, "The worse is over for you."

If only that were true.[76] What it does to you and those you love is the worse.

Mary DeMuth writes about this in her book, *Everything*:

> Growing up, I had a hard time believing my family loved me. Of course, part of this was my fault. Because of my insatiable need for love (I hadn't yet met Jesus), I placed high expectations on the adults in my life to fill every nook and cranny of my heart. When I failed, folks in my family not only withdrew but also shamed me, sometimes even ridiculing me for my failure. When this happened, I'd think something like, *If I fail, I'm rejected. So if I'm perfect, I'll prove to them that I am worthy of love.* Using this simple logic, I lived a lifelong vow to overwork, overimpress, overachieve… Achieving became my drug, my recognition, my insatiable need.[77]

I relate to this overachieving. This need to be perfect and to perform perfectly. This need for others to look at me as a shining star, admire me, respect me, love me—unconditionally. Just love me. Accept me. Want me. Tell me I'm okay.

Please.

Other effects of child abuse/neglect include[78]:

- Academic difficulties, attention problems, concentration problems
- Aggressive behavior, stealing
- Alcohol/drug abuse
- Anxiety, panic attacks, bad dreams, fears
- Depression, disassociation
- Eating disorders and failure to thrive

- Insomnia
- Running away
- Frequent injuries, cutting, repeated self-injury
- Risky sexual behaviors or sexual dysfunction
- Social withdrawing, shyness, fear of people or spaces
- Lying, manipulation
- Self-neglect
- Age-inappropriate behavior like thumb-sucking
- Suicide ideation or suicide

God can heal all of these things. (He can even raise the dead!). For Mary DeMuth, God has done amazing healing in her life. She writes, "The beautiful thing is that if a stranger met me today, she would not discern this story. God has so fully healed me from the past that most people have no idea about the devastation of my childhood. By God's sheer grace, they see joy, contentment, health, compassion, authenticity, and confidence. Not devastation. Not isolation. Not neglect. This is the power of Jesus to heal even the most broken life."[79]

While God has done miraculous, healing, delivering work in my life, and will continue to do so, recently someone told me that she could hardly believe everything I'd been through. "You could never tell that about you now, all that pain," she said. What a testimony to the power of Jesus Christ my Savior, Healer, and Deliverer! God can restore you and renew you, too, no matter what you've been through.

Stormie O'Martian shares her powerful story in *Stormie: A Story of Forgiveness and Healing* of triumphing over the horrific childhood abuse from her mother Virginia, who was diagnosed schizophrenic in Stormie's adulthood.

Her mother locked her in closets for hours, physically abused her, called her "crazy," a "whore" and a "liar," socially isolated her, kept a filthy house and yelled at Stormie if she tried to clean it, was paranoid and thought the FBI, the Mafia and others were after her, and one time acted as if she would stab her with a sharp knife, laughing at Stormie's fears. At night Virginia stayed awake, talking to imaginary people.

As an adult, Stormie was saved by faith in Christ and went through spiritual deliverance. She found keys to peace, wholeness, love, abundance, growth, ongoing deliverance, fruitfulness, and restoration. Those keys were:

- Daily reading the Bible and proclaiming it to refute Satan's lies
- Prayer
- Daily confession of sin
- Forgiveness
- Saying "yes" to God
- Praise and worship of God
- Fasting from food

Stormie realized just how far God had brought her when she was going to share her testimony with hard, angry-looking inmates at a prison and she told Him she just didn't think she could do this. He said, "I am a Redeemer. I make all things news. I can take all the pain, and the scars, and I can not only heal them, but I can make them count for something."

And He did.[80] For days Stormie spoke and ministered to the prisoners, who were still physically behind bars, but were set free spiritually and emotionally from the pain of their past by God's love.

God can do this in your life as well, no matter what others have done to you or you have done. His promises include healing and restoration.

Then they cried to the Lord in their trouble, and he saved them from their distress; he sent out his word and healed them, and delivered them from destruction. Let them thank the Lord for his steadfast love, for his wonderful works to humankind.[81]

## Chapter 3

# abortion
# you can't go to the ball

*"See that you do not despise one of these little ones. For I tell you that in heaven their angels always see the face of my Father who is in heaven."*
Matthew 18:10

In high school English class, I had to read a book that profoundly impacted me: *The Scarlet Letter* by Nathaniel Hawthorne.[82] It was set in seventeenth century Puritan Boston, and tells the story of Hester Prynne, who conceives a daughter through an adulterous affair and tries to create a new life of repentance and dignity. Its theme is legalism, sin, and guilt. After Hester's adultery is discovered, she is punished socially and is forced to wear a large, scarlet "A" on her chest, which is a symbol of her sin – a badge of shame, for everyone to see. (Why didn't the man have to wear a scarlet "A"? Just sayin'.)

One quote from the book stands out to me:

> "Ah, but," interposed, more softly, a young wife, holding a child by the hand, "let her cover the mark as she will, the pang of it will be always in her heart."

As humans, we sin each day; it is why we need a Savior, Jesus Christ. But there are some sins which have much more serious consequences than others. Some sins cause life-long regret and pain in the heart. Some sins people never forget—or let you forget. Someone who has habitually lied in the past will experience skepticism and distrust from others, even when he or she is telling the truth, because he/she has lied so much in the past.

If you commit adultery, it can have devastating, life-long consequences on your marriage and family. In fact, the list for how it can negatively impact you and others is quite long, and includes[84]:

- Loss of your spouse's friendship and others' friendships
- Loss of a sexual relationship with spouse
- Unbearable pain for the spouse
- Spouse or the "other" man/woman possibly doing something crazy (Remember the movie *Fatal Attraction* with Glenn Close and Michael Douglas? Powerful!)
- Spouse's distrust; continual strife and arguments in the marriage
- Unbearable pain for the children
- Children falling away from their Christian faith
- Public humiliation/ gossip from others
- Sexually transmitted disease/AIDS
- Loneliness/Guilt/Shame

There are some things that you can never take back. Adultery is one of them; abortion is another.

Abortion can't be undone. You have killed a child. You will never see that baby grow up, smile, laugh, crawl, walk, run, play, or fulfill his or her purpose for which God created that child. Like Cinderella told, "You can't go to the ball," when it was her destiny. You'll never hear the aborted child's sweet voice. You will never know that magnificent little person.

If you think I am being harsh and judgmental, I'm not. I've had three abortions. I know its great pain and regret. I also know God's complete forgiveness of my sin. Abortion is not the unforgiveable sin.[85] If you have had one (or more), He will forgive you if you ask Him to, if you have a relationship with Him through Jesus Christ. I believe that one day I will see my three babies in heaven. I believe all aborted babies (and miscarried babies) go to heaven. Those children are not punished for our sins.

**The Deception**

I was already saved when I had my first abortion and the two subsequent ones. But I bought the lie of abortion and was deceived that it was the answer to my fears. You may wonder, why would someone have an abortion – especially a Christian? At first you don't view abortion as a sin, or at least that is what you tell yourself.

Abortion is a lie. The world promises you that it's a solution to your distressing problem—an unexpected pregnancy. Women are deceived about what it is—the taking of human life. Murder.

When you are a young, single woman and you become pregnant out of wedlock, it is a terrifying thing. The first thoughts that run through your mind are, "Oh, no!", "What am I going to do?", and "What will my family and friends say?"

Today pregnancies before or outside of marriage are much more common, and with a fast-growing abandonment of Christian morals, the stigma is not as strong now as it used to be. But the fear and the shame for the pregnant woman still exist.

When you go to Planned Parenthood and some medical clinics, you are encouraged to get an abortion if you weren't planning the pregnancy and/or don't want the baby. Once you go into an abortion clinic, their job is to convince you that abortion is the right decision. They are trained to act sympathetic and understanding, and to play on your fears, especially financial ones. They tell you this will "get rid of the problem." It's a convincing lie –one of Satan's most powerful ones.

From an online article, "The Ex-Abortionists: Why They Quit," we read:

> Kathy Sparks described a skilled "counselor" at her clinic who would find what a woman's key pressure point was—perhaps a fear of telling her parents she was pregnant, perhaps money worries—and then "magnify it." She said that ninety-nine percent of the women who came in decided to have abortions. Joy Davis reported the careful training she received at her first clinic in Alabama: "I had to sit and listen to women answering the phone for at least a month before they would allow me to answer the phone....We had to find out very quickly what their problem was, play on that, and get them in that clinic for an abortion. We were very good salespeople."[86]
>
> Hellen Pendley's staff learned how to play on money fears by asking a woman who was ambivalent: "Do you know how expensive it is if you go through with this? Let me just tell you. . . . It's gonna [sic] cost you about $8,000 just to have [the child]. Now, where are you gonna [sic] get that kind of money?"[87]
>
> Pendley commented that "it's really pretty simple to bring someone around to your way of thinking if you can

manipulate what they've told you and use it against them. And that's exactly what we did."[88]

I became pregnant three different times by three different men and had three abortions over a ten-year span. I vaguely remember my second and third abortions. But because of trauma, my mind has mostly blocked out the memories of my first abortion.

The father of the first aborted baby didn't want me to have an abortion. He was in love with me. When I told him the news that I was pregnant, he said we could marry and be a family. He promised to provide for me and the baby the rest of our lives. He was actually excited and happy about it.

## Haunted

By that time, I was desperately trying to think of a way to break up with him to get away from him. He didn't know this. He was obsessed with me, had a temper, drank and did drugs. He was extremely jealous and possessive of me, and wouldn't leave me alone. I began to feel suffocated by him. I was afraid if I had his child (even if we never married), he would haunt me the rest of my life. I feared that I'd never be rid of him.

I didn't want to have an abortion. I believed it was morally wrong. But I was terrified. If I went through the pregnancy and didn't marry this man, how would I take care of this baby financially? I was already divorced with a young child, and temporarily living at home with my father to get back on my feet. I didn't want to put more financial and emotional stress on my dad by having another baby.

I told no one else but the father of the baby that I was pregnant, and called an abortion clinic in Florida to ask questions and make an appointment. I didn't dare have an abortion anywhere near the city where my father lived and he could possibly find out the news (my mother had passed away years before then).

My whole life I had often heard from my parents, "What will others think?" Others' opinions, not God's word, were the basis of my parents' morality, and for all they thought, said, and did. My father was well known as a successful businessman. He was heavily involved in and recognized with awards in a community service club. He had a sterling reputation.

I believed that my dad would be ashamed from his daughter's out-of-wedlock pregnancy. The fear of my father's disapproval and of causing him shame is what primarily drove my decision to have an abortion. The fear of my father was greater than my fear of God.

To make sure that daddy wouldn't find out that I was pregnant or that I'd had an abortion, I left the state to have it. He didn't know the doctors there. To this day, I have never told him. Maybe I am still afraid of his disapproval.

My boyfriend wanted the baby, but supported my decision. He gave me the money for the abortion and for my gas to drive to the clinic, because I didn't have the funds. I arranged for a babysitter for my daughter Heather and drove alone to Florida in my little car. My mind has blocked out the trip and the actual procedure; I don't remember any of it.

I do remember the physical pain after the abortion and wondering how I would be able to drive home. The staff gave me medication for pain to take when I returned home and to prevent infection. They told me to watch for symptoms of infection, following up with a doctor in two weeks.

They let me rest at the clinic in a bed for awhile, before releasing me on my own cognizance. I have a vague, sad memory of laying in the recovery bed, terrified, knowing I had just done something horribly wrong—and could never take it back.

Somehow after the staff released me, I made it back driving home. I hid what I'd done from everyone, including my father and Heather. I didn't tell Heather until she was grown, because I feared that she would stop loving me once she knew. I didn't want to be an ungodly example to her.

Like Hester's scarlet letter "A," I wore a badge of shame on my countenance, but told no one the truth. As a Christian, I felt like a hypocrite. I kept this horrible, dark secret deep inside of me, and didn't tell anyone about the abortion until eleven years later.

I admit that emotionally, I felt relieved that my "problem" was over—but guilty. Always guilty. And angry. Weeks after my trip to the abortion clinic, I broke up with my boyfriend—and began hating him, which bewildered him. It was easier to lash out at him in anger, than to acknowledge anger and hate at myself for what I'd done. He was a safe target.

The abortion haunted me. I could hardly live with myself. I was so ashamed, and felt guilty and fearful all the time. I was scared God was going to send me to hell for my sin. I became more depressed, anxious, and afraid. I began drinking heavily, experimenting with a few drugs, and became promiscuous. What, or who, was I running from?

Certainly God and myself.

I didn't realize I'd developed Post Abortion Syndrome (PAS).

## Post-Abortion Syndrome (PAS)

The symptoms of PAS can include:

- Guilt.
- Anxiety from the conflict of a woman's moral standards and her decision to abort.
- Psychological nmbing, to keep from feeling the pain of what happened and to keep emotions tightly in check. This also keeps women from forming and maintaining close relationships.
- Depression and suicidal thoughts. A study by the Elliot Institute revealed that 33 percent of post-abortive women who were surveyed said they'd rather die than go on.
- PAS symptoms around the anniversary of the abortion and the child's due date.
- Flashbacks of the abortion; nightmares of the lost, dismemberbed, or crying babies.
- Preoccupation with pregnancy again or anxiety about being unable to ever get pregnant again or carry a baby to term.
- Bonding with children or future children; devaluing them; trying to become the "perfect mother"; being overprotective.
- Eating disorders like anorexia, bulimia, or excessive weight gain, which can reduce the changes of becoming pregnant again.
- Alcohol and drug abuse.
- Self-destructive behaviors, like abusive relationships, promiscuity, or hurting herself physically.
- Brief reactive psychosis—a break with reality due to the stress from the abortion. (This is rare, but can happen.)[89]

Abortion does not solve any problem. Instead, it creates more serious problems—and life-long regret.[90]

## Abortion #2 – Running Again

You'd think that I would've sincerely repented and learned something from the physical, spiritual, and emotional pain of the first abortion. Yet, foolishly, I went on to have two more.

I'm still not sure exactly why I had any of my abortions, except that I felt desperate and afraid. My decision to abort my babies was primarily motivated by fear of people's disapproval (especially my father's) and fears over finances, which I was already struggling with as a single mom. Most women base their decision to abort for several reasons, the most common being lack of money or lack of readiness to start or expand a family.[91]

After my first abortion, I continued to search for fulfillment. Everywhere I went, I looked for healing, restoration, and most of all love—love in all the wrong places. It was a God-void, a God-hole.

One night, after drinking too much beer and crying about an emotionally-distanced man with whom I'd become obsessed, I turned for help to my platonic, male, best friend—and wound up sleeping with him. That night, I knew it was a mistake as soon as it happened. In daylight hours, this man wasn't physically attractive in the least to me and I felt repulsed that I'd had sex with him. Somehow I knew I was pregnant immediately from this one drunken decision that had affected my judgment. The next morning, I was running again.

Several weeks later, when I saw the "positive" line on two home pregnancy tests (two to make sure), I called my friend and told him, letting him know right away that I'd have an abortion. Ironically, this man didn't want me to have an abortion, either. He asked why he didn't have a say in the matter. That is a legitimate question. Feminists talk about the woman's rights, but what about the father's rights? Most of all, what about the baby's right to live?

As abortion survivor Gianna Jessen says, "If abortion is merely about women's rights, what about mine? There was not a radical feminist standing up and yelling about how my rights were being violated that day; in fact, my life was being snuffed out in the name of women's rights."[92]

Gianna also challenges us, "It is a battle between life and death—what side are you on?"[93]

I met Gianna one time when the staff of the pro-life pregnancy center where I volunteered as a lay counselor took a trip together to hear her speak. She's beautiful, intelligent, funny, deep, wise, and a devout follower of Jesus Christ. There is an other-world, holy presence about her. God's Spirit of righteousness emanates from her. I felt so convicted of my sins of abortion being near her, that I wanted to run out of the room.

I gave lame excuses to my friend for "needing" to have an abortion. Number one, I didn't want a baby, not now. And I wasn't in love with him; I was obsessed about another man. Number two, I didn't have the finances to raise another child and neither did he. And number three, although I didn't tell him this, I didn't want this man haunting me the rest of my life because I'd had his child. But it all really boiled down to sin and my selfishness.

Our friendship took a fast nosedive as I demanded that he give me the money for the abortion and drive me to the abortion clinic in Florida, where I'd set up an appointment by phone. He was in the military and didn't make a big salary, so taking time off from work and forking out the money for an abortion was difficult. (I believe it was about $200 then; it's now between $350 and $500 for a first trimester abortion and even more for advanced pregnancies.)
By the time he had scrounged up the money from his paycheck and from borrowing money from friends, my pregnancy had advanced

into the second trimester. I was gaining weight more rapidly with this pregnancy, and my abdomen was noticeably rounding, my jeans becoming tighter.

I had a feeling this would be a big baby, and sensed it was a boy. I had sensed the first baby was a girl. But I pushed these thoughts aside, only wanting "to get rid of the problem." I was afraid if I waited much longer, I wouldn't be able to have an abortion as many clinics don't perform last trimester abortions. (Today it's legal to have an abortion into the last trimester.)

Abortionists charge more money, the further you are into the pregnancy. Somehow my friend had to come up with more money for the procedure.

## A Hardened Heart

The memories from this abortion are hazy as well. I recall the abortion clinic's dingy, dirty, oppressive waiting room. I remember teenage girls and women reading magazines with anxious pale faces, not looking at or speaking with each other. The silence was ominous. We were all trying not to think of what we were about to do.

My name was called. My palms became sweaty and my heart was drumming fast in my chest as I went through the doors to the back area of the clinic. You have to take a pregnancy test for the staff to make sure you're pregnant. I wanted to run away, but I didn't want to be pregnant.

After talking with a "counselor" who explained the abortion procedure and potential risks and answered my few questions, I had to put on a thin gown in a cold room, like you do in doctors' offices. Why was I doing this again?

I tried not to think about God and the grief He was feeling over my decision. Yet God was right there. He saw it all, and I believe He wept—both for my baby and for me.

I knew abortion was morally wrong, but I hardened my heart and went ahead with it. All I could think of at that time was that I could not have this man's baby, and that my father mustn't ever find out about this. I was already practiced in keeping secrets, from my childhood abuse. Later I would keep more secrets, from myself and others.

I remember the doctor and his staff talking and laughing about a football game during the procedure, and the rage I felt inside. I wanted to scream at them: "Who cares about the football game? What about what I'm going through here?" Tears filled my eyes, and the nurse patted my hand to comfort me.

This abortion was harder physically on me than the first one; I was in a great deal of physical pain, probably because I was into the second trimester. I remember lying in the recovery room in pain, and how surprised I was to see other patients in the room. We were all lying in single cots on sterile white sheets, bleeding, some crying, some emotionally numb. One of the ways a post-abortive woman copes is to numb herself—to not ever think about it, to not feel. The guilt is instantly overwhelming.

The memory that stands out to me from this abortion is how cold I felt physically (I stay hot most of the time, so this is unusual). I also remember feeling not just guilt, but a panicky sense of doom and a terror of going to hell for what I'd just done. I lived with those feelings daily for many more years.

Never feeling assured of my salvation, I went to church altars often after I'd had the second abortion, getting "saved" again and again.

One of my best friends, Wendy, was very puzzled over this, asking me why when I was already saved. Jesus' work was finished at the cross, she said. It was hard to explain to her. Many post-abortive women and men battle feeling condemnation and the fear of God's judgment, not understanding God's unconditional love and forgiveness. The fear of going to hell after having an abortion is tormenting.

**Sleep was Bliss**

After the second abortion, I was given medication by the abortion clinic staff for pain and to prevent infection, and was instructed to follow up with a doctor back home. On the way home, my friend (the father) drove and I slept on and off in the car. For several days after the abortion, I stayed at his house, sleeping, knocked out on pain medication.

Sleep was bliss, because I didn't have to think about the abortion or anything else in my life. It was my escape from reality. Sometimes I still feel this way, whenever I'm emotionally struggling. Other than God's presence and the ocean, sleep is the only place where I feel true, deep peace. Sleep, like the beautiful ocean, is a gift.

> The sea does not reward those who are too anxious, too greedy, or too impatient. To dig for treasures shows not only impatience and greed, but lack of faith. Patience, patience, patience, is what the sea teaches. Patience and faith. One should lie empty, open, choiceless as a beach—waiting for a gift from the sea.[94]

After the second abortion, I'd taken several days off work to recover. One day my father found out that I wasn't at work when he called the office to talk with me, and later questioned me about it. I told him that I had to go to a "specialist" in Florida for a "medical problem," but was okay now. He didn't probe further—probably he really didn't want to know.

By God's grace, I was physically healing from the abortion. Some women experience the following physical effects, even with a one-time abortion[95]:

- Spotting
- Heavy bleeding
- Infections or sepsis
- Torn cervix
- Perforation of the uterus
- Damage to other organs
- Death from abortions

Yes, I could have died! No one told me this when I had my abortions. The abortion clinic's staff downplays the risks and focus on your fears to get your money.

My body was recovering, but unconfessed guilt, shame, and anger were forming a hard, protective callous around my heart that would be difficult to penetrate by others in the years ahead. Keeping others at an arm-length's distance was the only way to keep my secrets carefully tended and safe.

The emotional strain of hiding from others, especially my father who seemed to know things without anyone telling him, was exhausting. I wore a public mask, smiling, pretending, but inside me emotions spun, like the gravitational strong pull of a black hole in space. Sometimes black holes collapse in themselves. I felt I'd collapse soon.

It was only a matter of a couple of weeks after the second abortion that I suddenly and completely cut off my friendship with the father of this aborted baby. I told him in a rage over the phone that I wanted nothing more to do with him and to leave me alone. He was bewildered, confused, and hurt at my sudden anger. My self-hatred was being poured out like black lava on him, and on others who would cross my path later. The castle walls around my heart grew thicker, a fortress that kept me from receiving or giving love, except with my family and a few close friends.

No one was going to get close enough to find out my dark secrets. Thinking my "problem" over, I then decided to focus on my education and career. Again, I buried the pain and guilt, never telling anyone my dark secret. I wore shame like an old, raggedy winter coat, my heart stone cold, my soul in anguish. I experienced what Saint John of the Cross wrote in his poem, *The Dark Night of the Soul*. Sainte Terese of Lisieux, a nineteenth century French Carmelite nun, allegedly wrote of her own experience, "If you only knew what darkness I am plunged into."

Peace eluded me. I didn't realize Jesus was the embodiment of peace and love.

Maybe a good career making more money would help. I began waitressing and going back to school. During the week, I'd go to school from 8 a.m. to 3 p.m., learning filing and shorthand and improving my typing speed. On weekends, I'd go to work at the hotel restaurant, drink a coke and eat bacon and toast sandwiches, and count my tips at the end of the day, putting some money in the bank at my father's sage advice. This would certainly help me as a single mom to provide better for my daughter Heather.

**Desperately Searching for Love**

My father was pleased that I was getting more education, especially something business-related and "practical" (unlike becoming a writer), which could help me become more self-supporting…and maybe move out of his house. I studied hard and made As, but my heart wasn't in school. I had roller-coaster emotions, was bored, restless and unfulfilled, and partied on weekends with friends to escape thinking about anything, especially my abortions.

My father drank alcohol, too, but it was my late hours arriving home that concerned and angered him. He said he never knew if I was dead or alive, and asked me to call if I would be getting home late. Those partying days added unnecessary years of worry to my father's life, and many gray hairs (his coal-black hair seemed to turn silver overnight!), which I now deeply regret.

Becoming a parent helps you to understand and appreciate your own parents so much more. Years later after I moved out, my heart smitten, I apologized to daddy in a letter for causing him so much worry and trouble. He wrote me back, saying he had forgiven me of everything and to please forgive him also of any way he had hurt me.

I never meant to hurt God, my father, or myself. I should've stayed at home, spending time with my little girl, Heather. Even now, remembering my selfish immaturity and how often I left Heather in my younger sister Maria's care on weekend nights, it pains my heart. I'm so grateful God protected my life and I didn't die, and for His forgiveness. Now I know that I was just lonely, very confused, and running from God, but that is no excuse for my sins.

The truth is, I've had to grow up with Heather, since I had her when I was just nineteen years old. I'm so thankful that she's forgiven my sins in the past and that today we are not just mother and daughter, but great friends.

While I pursued my education, I still kept thinking that finding the right man would solve all my problems—someone who would just love me, despite myself. I was so lonely. While attending vocational training school to become a secretary, I met and became involved with a man who had a troubled marriage. He left his wife to be with me and we moved into a rental house together.

I realized too late that he was jealous, controlling, possessive and verbally abusive, much like the father of my first aborted baby. (Throughout my twenties, I was drawn to men who would physically or verbally abuse me. I now realize this is because of my childhood abuse. Many women in domestic violence situations grew up in homes where there was excessive violence or turbulence. They may have blamed themselves for the dysfunction or unhappiness.[96] They often think they don't deserve better treatment.)

When he drank beers after work, he'd start getting mean. I began to worry that Heather and I were unsafe with him, and felt like Heather and I had to walk on eggshells around him. Heather began to act fearful toward him, even though he had never physically hit her. He told me I was too "easy" on her as a parent, and was verbally harsh with her for misbehavior. I've learned since then to pay attention to your gut. My gut was telling me to get out of this relationship.

He began accusing me of having affairs, which I wasn't having. His guilty conscience over leaving his wife was eating at him. After he would drink and berate me or Heather, he'd feel contrite and apologize the next day.

After months of living in this toxic environment, I packed my belongings, put Heather in the car, and left, moving back home with my dad, feeling between a rock and a hard place. Would I never find what I was looking for?

He stalked me for awhile. One night I was driving down the road, and he drove up beside me—apparently having followed me. Shouting through his open car window and pointing, he asked me to pull over into a parking lot for a minute. I felt wary of him, but rolled down the window for him to talk to me from his car.

He said, "Babe, I just want to thank you. Thank you for breaking up with me! This situation really opened my eyes to how I need to change my life! So thank you!"

I looked into his eyes and despite his smile, I saw hurt. I also felt he was emotionally unstable. His words made me uneasy, like he was on the verge of a psychotic break and he might go postal on me. I said okay and hurriedly drove off. I felt relieved that I was out of the relationship for good.

I desperately needed to feel God's love and to find peace with Him. I thought of God as an angry God, ready to throw me into hell. In my early twenties, I had sought Jesus in the Catholic Church and had converted to Roman Catholicism. After I left this man, I went back to the Catholic Church, which I'd been attending recently, to go to confession.

Confession is never fun, but it had always given me temporary relief. But as soon as I told the priest about my two abortions—which I'd never told anyone about—his eyes grew enormous and his face was horrified.

I knew my abortions were sin and were wrong, but his reaction made me realize how emotionally and spiritually numb I had become. It shook me to the core, and strengthened my fear and belief that I was going to hell.

For a moment, I thought the priest was going to order me out of the church. I could tell he was trying to cope with his own emotions about this and wasn't sure how to respond to me.

Maybe I was the first person who had ever confessed to having an abortion—or two abortions—to him. Women often are so ashamed of their abortions, they don't tell anyone. The secrecy is part of why some post-abortive women or men are never healed.

I also told the priest that I had left my fiancé' because things were not working out, and to my surprise and anger, he urged me to reconsider because "he's a good Catholic man."

I felt that he wouldn't receive anything I said about this man's verbal abuse, because he disapproved of me for having the abortions. I puzzled over how this priest could approve of our relationship and potential marriage, knowing that this man had left his wife for me—and that we were living in sin together, not married! "Thou shalt not commit adultery" (the relationship I had with this man) was in the same Ten Commandments as "Thou shalt not kill" (abortion).[97]

The priest finally granted absolution to me (which actually only God can do!), and told me to say the prayers of "Hail Mary" for my "penance."

*Promises in the dark.*

I felt relief at having told someone finally, but still didn't feel clean. I wasn't clean! I had never sincerely repented for my abortions. I was terrified of going to hell, but I hadn't come face to face with my own sins and how they'd grieved God and hurt myself and others. I was much like Esau who regretted what he'd done and cried for his birthright, but he did not seek true godly repentance.

## Damaged Goods

Abortion causes men and women to feel like damaged goods.

> If you walked into any store today you would find a corner, way in the back, which has a pile of damaged goods. These are products that have been dropped or chipped or soiled in some way and are not fit for sale. Only perfect items have the value that allows them to be displayed on the shelf. The damaged products are really good for nothing and typically get tossed out at the end of the day or sent back to the factory.[98]

> Maybe this is how you feel about your life. Maybe you have been divorced, not once but twice or even more. Maybe you have been adopted or had an abortion. Maybe you have lost a job that you thought you were made for. Or maybe you have been sexually abused. Any one of these life events can leave you feeling like damaged goods. In your mind, you don't deserve to be placed on the shelf with "normal" people. You are convinced that you are damaged and, because of that, you go through life anticipating rejection at every turn.[99]

This describes exactly how I felt. I didn't believe I was worthy of being treated well because of my childhood abuse and the abortions. Maybe those feelings of unworthiness are partly why I married my second husband, an abuser. I didn't see the danger signs until it was almost too late.

## Give Me Light!

In my book, *The Hands Of A Woman: Everyday Women In Everyday Battles*[100], I shared about my second abusive marriage, when my ex-husband verbally and physically battered me and my daughter Heather. He nearly killed Heather and she had to have immediate brain surgery.

He lied to me that she fell down the stairs while I was at the grocery store. I chose to believe him, not wanting to believe that anyone would hurt a child like that, despite one previous incidence of his physically abusing her and one situation of abuse of our cat before that.

I'd stayed, fearful and confused, after the first incident with Heather, because he cried like a baby, begging forgiveness and swearing it'd never happen again. After he left and we divorced, it took me a long time to forgive myself for staying with him after the first incidence. I'd wanted to believe that he'd never hit her again.

*Promises in the dark.*

In the second incident of abuse, God had great mercy and she lived. I came home from the store, found her in bed with her eyes rolled back in her head, limp, and barely breathing, and began screaming hysterically. I ran downstairs, fell to my knees on the floor, and grabbed the carpet, screaming over and over because I thought she was dead. I felt as if my mind would snap from the trauma. He lied that she had fallen down the stairs, put us both in the car, and rushed her to the E.R. She was in my arms in the front seat of our car, with my ex-husband driving like a mad man.

On the way to the hospital, I looked down at my limp, pale, beautiful child and cried out to God, "Lord, have mercy! Have mercy!" Suddenly, the wind of the Holy Spirit blew through that car and Heather took a breath. I believe she was dead or almost dead up to that point.

The staff at the E.R. was incompetent and said they thought she would be all right, but they'd keep her overnight for observation. I adamantly said no; I knew, looking into her hazel eyes that seemed to be looking into some other world, that something was terribly wrong. If I had listened to them instead of to my gut, she'd be dead. We immediately transferred her to a larger hospital, where her x-rays revealed a hematoma (bleeding) in the brain. She was taken into surgery right away, which lasted for several hours.

God orchestrated a divine appointment for me in the waiting room; a compassionate pastor sat beside me during the entire surgery, praying for her and for me. All I could do was read the Bible, pray, and weep, physically shaking in terror that she might die any moment. The pastor held my hand and prayed for faith for me and healing for Heather.

I don't know what I would've done without that pastor beside me. My then-husband was there, but he was no help to me emotionally or spiritually, pacing up and down the halls, talking loudly to others, and saying he was hungry. I couldn't eat. I felt like I'd throw up any minute. I wanted him to leave.

A dark suspicion about him was growing in my mind that I had to keep fighting, but I didn't dare voice it. At this moment, all that mattered was for Heather to be okay.

When the surgeon came out of the operating room, telling us it had gone well and she was going to be okay, my then-husband finally broke down, leaning his hands on the wall, his head bowed, crying hard.

I looked over at him, surprised and puzzled, because I'd never seen him cry before. Maybe in reality, he was thanking God for His mercy. He has never confessed this abuse to me, or anyone else that I know of, to this day.

By this point, I was in shock and greatly relieved, thanking God, the surgeon, and the pastor who had sat with me in the waiting room. My father and his girlfriend, an R.N., were on their way to the hospital from a city several hours away.

Although the doctors initially questioned my then-husband several times about what happened to her when she was first transferred there, the staff didn't report it to social services as child abuse. I assume it is because he was a well-known deputy sheriff in town—after all, he was someone who upheld the law every day, right? I have forgiven him, but I am extremely thankful to have him out of our lives forever.

Through surgery, followed by several months of recovery, Heather completely and miraculously healed from her brain hematoma with no negative physical side effects. Today she's a beautiful, spiritually gifted, vibrantly healthy, happy woman, the mother of two beautiful little girls, a chiropractor's assistant, and a fulltime college student. You would never know that she'd been through this trauma. To God be the glory!

Yes, I should have known that he'd done this, but I was in deep denial. There was one time of foreboding before we married. Sadly, I closed my eyes to it, marrying him anyway and making one of the biggest, most regretful mistakes of my life.

While we were dating, one night he became angry with me because he thought I was acting emotionally distant with him (rejection seemed to be the trigger for his rages), and loudly verbally abused me in front of the patrons, to my shock. Embarrassed and stunned, I walked out alone from the restaurant where we were having dinner, crying.

Another couple in the restaurant had observed the scene, and the woman came up to me outside, asking if I was okay. I said yes, and we talked a little. When she found out that we were engaged, she said, "Honey, if he acts this way before you marry him, he will act this way and worse afterward. You really need to think about this before you make a commitment."

She was merely echoing my own thoughts, but I pushed them down into the deep recesses of my mind, excusing his behavior and thinking it was my fault somehow.

He walked up to her then and told her to mind her own #*!%! business, and ordered me in the car immediately. She said something back to him, but by then, I was growing uneasy about his sudden, angry behavior and didn't want to provoke him further. Unfortunately, I didn't listen to her sage advice and married him anyway.

It was the only time he showed his temper before our wedding. He apologized profusely the next day, something that would become a pattern in our marriage when he would go into a rage. He'd buy me flowers, an expensive gift, or romance me somehow – and I was an idiot for believing him and ever being with him. If something like this has happened to you, I beg you to wait and carefully watch behavior before marrying. I thought this single incidence of verbal abuse was maybe just a fluke, and we would live happily ever after.

*Promises in the dark.*

For awhile after the Las Vegas wedding, it seemed like we were happy. I'd attend college classes during the daytime, pick up Heather from school, and he'd come home in the evenings from working all day at the sheriff's department. Then we'd usually go out to eat somewhere nice, because I didn't know how to cook much then and he loved to eat (and now I dislike cooking— something I'll talk more about later!).

Occasionally we'd go over to his friends' houses and we'd have supper with them. The wives' southern cooking with fried chicken or meat loaf, mashed potatoes, squash, butterbeans, fresh cut tomatoes, and cucumbers—with some kind of sweet berry pie or cake for dessert—made him happy, at least for the moment.

His closest friends in town—and substitute parents—were a couple who owned a funeral home and lived in an apartment right over the home. My second ex-husband's mother had abandoned and left him, something he never got over. When he was a child, his father beat him, but they had reconciled after he was grown.

The funeral home couple's respect and love for him was balm to his wounded soul. I thought they were very strange people; they just acted, for lack of a better word, odd. We'd sit on the front porch of the funeral home in big rocking chairs, talking and drinking Cokes. Then he'd have to go to work.

Sometimes he'd have night duty and would patrol the town all night long. Over time, the night shifts became more frequent. It seemed that he was working unusually long hours, both days and nights, with a schedule I could never keep up with from him. Although I wondered about it, I'm an introvert and prefer solitude, so I didn't complain. Sometimes I missed it just being me and Heather, and I missed my family, who I rarely saw anymore. My father had warned me to give my engagement period with this man more time because things were going too fast, but I dismissed the concerns. How I wish I'd listened to that woman outside the restaurant and my father now!

After our Las Vegas wedding at a little white chapel, my then-husband would often buy me fresh flowers, tell me every day he loved me, and would teasingly call me "Marjorie" after the writer Marjorie Kinnan Rawlings, because I often read the book *Cross Creek* and wanted to be a successful, famous writer like her. He bought me a typewriter to write my first book, and encouraged me to write every day.

He made the money, paid the bills, and gave me "shopping money" to go buy me and Heather pretty clothes and shoes. My first husband, Heather's biological father, was years behind in child support. After our divorce, he only worked sometimes, while I had to work full-time to support Heather. He and I had been poor our entire marriage. In my second marriage, I didn't have to work outside the home; I went to school full-time. For the first time in years, I didn't have to worry about finances—but at what price?

My second husband flirted often with me in our marriage—and with every other woman in town. Even with the funeral home owner's wife, who was old enough to be his mother. Her husband would just laugh about it, as if it was a boyish antic.

He was, in fact, the town's most eligible bachelor when I married him. I don't think there was any woman, single or married, who he hadn't slept with there.

It was the town gossip for months when our engagement and wedding were announced in the paper; everyone was shocked that he was "finally settling down." Probably bets were laid down as to how long it would last. I tried to tell myself frequently when he flirted with women that it was me he loved; after all, he had married me, not them.

*Promises in the dark.*

He was bold about the flirting, to the point of being what my mother would've termed "vulgar." His conversations with women were peppered with sexual innuendoes, disguised as "only joking." But his constant flirting and hints of sex with other women made me very uncomfortable and irritated me.

Like Scarlet O'Hara, he had more charm than anyone should be allowed. He would've made a perfect politician with his smooth voice and cheesy, fake smile…yet I still married him, believing there was more depth underneath the surface. I dismissed my worries about the women, concentrating on taking care of Heather and my college studies, trying to soothe myself that it was just his "outgoing, friendly personality."

I had my daughter, I was pursuing my education, I was married, and I had a cat. Yet something was missing in my life. I couldn't put my finger on it. I began attending Catholic church with Heather, but my ex-husband wasn't interested in going with me.

Things began to change in our relationship. It was hardly noticeable at first, then I felt as if I was living with Dr. Jekyll and Mr. Hyde.[101]

After several months of marriage, I began to notice that he often seemed agitated and emotionally distant when he came home. His moods would grow brooding, darker, and he constantly and loudly criticized me and Heather. We both began to feel as if we had to walk on eggshells around him so his hair-trigger temper wouldn't be set off. When he arrived home from work, my stomach would have knots. Heather physically tensed around him, and her fear of him began to make me feel anxious.

I'd only dated this man a few months during my college summer internship at a newspaper before we married. I really didn't know him very well, but had rashly said yes to his proposal after he passionately pursued and romanced me with flattery, red roses, expensive dinners, and gifts.

He flashed money around, making me and others think he was wealthy, despite his middle-income-class job as a deputy sheriff. But the way he spent money on himself, me, and others, as if he didn't have a concern in the world, fooled me and the whole town. For all we knew, he was a millionaire.

As a poor single mom for so many years, I confess that the idea of not having to struggle financially any more if we married was very appealing, plus the way he made me believe that he thought I was the moon and stars to him. I'd never had this kind of attention before. Now I realize this man was just a "player." He'd acted this way with every other woman in his life, but he was dangerous.

The newspaper editor warned me when she found out that we were engaged that I should get to know him better first before marriage, and to talk to his ex-fiancé about why she broke up with him. I dismissed that idea, thinking the woman was a fool. Later I found out from her that it was because of his violent temper.

But other than the one incident at the restaurant, he kept his temper hidden from me while we dated. After we married, I began noticing his short fuse and unpredictable moods. His displeasure with me and his life grew — that I didn't know how to cook, I needed to keep up with washing the laundry every day, the apartment was too small and crowded, all I did all day long was suck on Cokes and not work — and if I kept eating BLTs (bacon, lettuce, and tomato sandwiches), he said, I was going to get fat. It was okay for him to eat BLTs, and he was far more overweight than I was. When I got visibly angry at his fat remark, he laughed and said he was just kidding.

The only thing that seemed to make him really happy was going out to dinner and having a thick, juicy, rare steak or being with his friends, many of whom were women he'd slept with, so I wasn't thrilled about spending time with them, nice as they were. I wasn't sure what the marriage problem was, but focused on my child and my college studies. Classes were getting harder and I was beginning to have a hard time concentrating on homework. He began complaining about that, too—that I always had my nose in my books and didn't pay enough attention to him.

After we'd been married for several months, I wanted to get myself and Heather a cat for our apartment duplex and we found a place which sold registered Siamese kittens, which Heather and I fell in love with instantly. I picked out a female one that we named "Victoria" and nicknamed her "Torie."

From the start, he seemed jealous of the attention and love I gave her. He wanted her litter box cleaned daily, if not several times a day, and complained it made our apartment stink. His resentment toward her grew daily.

Torie didn't seem to like him (animal instinct?) and would claw and bite him if he attempted to pet her, which wasn't often. Looking back, I think he was probably doing the petting just for show. When she bit him, he'd cuss at her. I began to feel fearful he might hit or hurt her.

One day I came home and saw Torie limping hard around the apartment. She was injured. I was horrified and began crying; he said that she had bitten him really hard and he "overreacted" and hit her. I think he probably threw her against a wall.

He seemed quite contrite after this, begging my and Heather's forgiveness, and promising it'd never happen again. She completely healed physically, but my and Heather's fear of him was growing.

I don't know why I married him or stayed with him after he hurt Torie. This incident with Torie was the first big red flag to what was coming—three incidences of abuse with Heather, with the second one resulting in her having brain surgery and the third one being the end of our marriage.

Shortly after Heather's brain surgery, I found out he was having an affair when the woman called our apartment duplex. I asked why she was calling him, and she told me they'd been seeing each other for awhile, shortly after we had married, and had kissed. I asked her if they had slept with each other, and she became quiet, laughed and said no. She then said, "But I just thought you should know."

I didn't believe her that he'd been seeing her. This man loved me!

*Promises in the dark.*

I thought she was lying. She said she thought I'd say that and played a tape of a phone conversation with her and him. Toward the end of the tape, he said he had to go, because "Beth had just driven up and was home." I felt like someone had punched me in the gut and felt sickened by the betrayal.

After confronting him when he came home and he ruefully admitted it was true, I was enraged and left him for a few days, with Heather. She seemed happy and relieved we had left, but I was an emotional mess and cried for days. I came back when he begged me to come home, saying he had cut off the relationship with his ex-girlfriend forever. He loved me, he said. He'd never loved any woman like me and he didn't know what came over him. He decided we'd move to the mid-west for a "fresh start." Maybe now we could live happily ever after.
*Promises in the dark.*

After we moved to Kansas, one morning when I woke up, I found out that he'd slapped Heather on the cheek. We began arguing over this. As I was getting my shoes for me and Heather to leave, he slammed my head into the side of a closet, bloodying my nose, then hurriedly left when I called the police. When he came home hours later, I demanded that he move out. He willingly left home and the state to go back South, where he'd been born and raised. I immediately filed papers to divorce him. I never saw him again.

Months later, after Heather felt safe enough with him permanently gone, she told me that her head injury hadn't been an accident—that he had hit her and then she didn't remember anything after that. I cried hard for months (and still do at times), imagining the terror she'd been feeling all this time, living with him. I reported it to my therapist. By this time, he had left the state and authorities took no criminal action against him. I don't know why they didn't pursue it. Now I'm just relieved this monster is out of our lives.

## Searching For a Safe Shore

After my second divorce, I thought I was through with men. I just needed to take care of me and Heather. I got a good job at an insurance company, was quickly promoted from mail clerk to executive secretary (doing word processing for seven executives), and began attending college again full-time, changing my major from journalism to psychology. I decided that I'd become a therapist, helping abused women and children. Now I thought that a higher education was "the answer" for my life issues.

> *Have you ever been at sea in a dense fog, when it seemed as if a tangible white darkness shut you in and the great ship, tense and anxious, groped her way toward the shore with plummet and sounding-line, and you waited with beating heart for something to happen? I was like that ship before my education began, only I was without compass or sounding line, and no way of knowing how near the harbor was. "Light! Give me light!" was the wordless cry of my soul, and the light of love shone on me in that very hour.*
>
> *~ Helen Keller ~*

Maybe, like Helen, I was trying to find solutions to my internal demons through the college psychology classes, to understand myself better, to find a safe shore from the dangerous current that I was swimming in. During this time, I also sought Christian counseling for myself and Heather to begin dealing with the pain of our past.

For five years I met weekly, sometimes twice a week, with my counselor Darrell, who I believe was a gift from God. During these hourly sessions I cried constantly, poured out my heart, and held onto him like a lifeline. He encouraged me that I was going to make it, believed in me, and affirmed God's gifts in me and His purpose for my life.

During my counseling, I processed the traumatic memories of my childhood, at times feeling as if my life were unraveling out of control. I wanted to find the matrix, the origin that held the answers to my many questions.

In the movie *The Matrix* with Keanu Reeves and Laurence Fishburne, I understood this sentence by Morpheus: "What you know you can't explain, but you feel it. You've felt it your entire life, that there's something wrong with the world. You don't know what it is, but it's there, like a splinter in your mind, driving you mad."

The splinter was the horrific sexual and physical abuse that had been done to me by people I loved and trusted, which they denied vehemently. Memories I'd repressed my whole life. But I'd felt the splinter. It was there. It had really happened and had robbed my innocent childhood and my entire life.

I was becoming increasingly suicidal and fearful as I worked through traumatic childhood memories in weekly therapy sessions.

Darrell became concerned and recommended that I voluntarily admit myself into a hospital for a few days to receive intensive therapy sessions.

There is a social stigma attached to psychiatric hospital admissions. I've battled fear writing about it in this book, not wanting people to judge me or think less of me—even Christians (or maybe *especially* Christians!). When I talked to my sister Maria about it on the phone today, I said I was thinking about deleting the parts about my hospitalizations in this book…or any book, for that matter. She said, "If you do that, you are still operating in the secrecy of your childhood. People who have been in the hospital or who are going into the hospital need to hear this. They need hope…the hope from this book!"

If you have ever been down the dark road of depression, you understand what I've been through. If you haven't, you don't ever want to go there.

I felt desperate for help. I was afraid I was going to succeed in killing myself, and then what would happen to Heather? Who would take care of her? I felt horribly guilty and berated myself for even thinking of doing this, after all Heather had been through—but my own emotions were a roller coaster. I was falling apart from anxiety and depression. I felt as if my life were folding in on me, like a house of cards collapsing.

Who would take care of Heather if I went into the hospital for intense therapy? My family of origin had abandoned us and I had few real friends.

Heather's babysitters helped me with taking care of Heather while I was undergoing intensive therapy in the hospital. It was one of many voluntary hospital admissions through five years of counseling.

I have many regrets over not being there physically or emotionally for Heather in her younger years, first in my twenties, partying, and then later from the hospitalizations. I was looking for help and answers to this maze called life...answers I didn't find behind prison-like hospital walls...answers that eluded me in group therapy sessions, art therapy, music therapy, talk therapy...answers I looked for in prescription pills to lift my mood, pills to help me sleep, pills to calm my anxiety.

There was no answer pill. Where was my safe haven? Where was Heather's? I couldn't bear being apart from my precious child and felt terrible guilt being away from her. I felt like a horrible, bad mother and cried a lot from the guilt.

The hospital stays actually made me more anxious, but I was able to have more intense counseling sessions with my doctor and my therapist...i.e., longer "talk" therapy.

We talked about my childhood, the abortions, my previous abusive marriage, my faith in God, my daughter Heather, doing things for fun, setting new goals for my life.

But it was so hard and scary being there. I'd never been around anyone mentally ill who had schizophrenia, bipolar disorder or other psychiatric problems. I observed at the hospital patients who yelled, cursed, acted sexually inappropriate, physically fought staff, refused food, and watched a lot of TV. Mostly I journaled, went to art therapy, slept a lot, tried to get away with not eating much (I had borderline anorexia), walked the grounds to admire nature outdoors, and talked to very few people, hiding in my room away from the noise and chaos.

My brother came to visit me once in the hospital, and as he looked around, he said, "You don't belong here. You're not crazy like these people." But when I tried to tell him why I was there—"There are some things about our family you don't know. Daddy..."- and he held up his hand to stop me and wouldn't listen. He knew I wasn't mentally ill, but it was easier to pretend I was "just crazy" than to accept the truth of my childhood abuse.

Hospital wards were an extremely frightening place. But I admit I met some interesting people there and learned a lot about what pain can do to people. Candy, a blonde-haired wisp of a girl, who was determined to starve herself until she just disappeared, because her father had raped her since she was a toddler. "The Edge," a young man who thought he was Jesus coming back in the Rapture. Tim, who drank so much water that he became sick and vomited, and was put on water restriction.

Chris, a flamboyant homosexual with a curly black afro, who frequently threatened the therapist in our group therapy sessions that he had plans to kill himself and when he did, he would definitely succeed...and nobody was going to stop him when he made up his mind to do it. She'd narrow her eyes at him to determine if he was bluffing, and he'd look back evenly at her, with an arrogant smile on his face, his nose raised in pride. Chris had been sexually abused as a child. Threatening suicide made him feel powerful.

Gloria, who had a psychotic breakdown after she was raped, thought that she was a TV news reporter covering a rape, and had to be hospitalized. She was a beautiful girl with a loud, vivacious laugh. She was released within a couple of days after "doing well" on her prescribed anti-psychotic medication. What the staff didn't know is that she was giving out the prescription narcotic drug Vicodin to other patients, I think in exchange for money.

Another patient in a different and calmer environment hospital was a gorgeous young woman, long blonde hair, blue eyes, tall, slender, the daughter of wealthy parents, looking very together on the outside, but who chose to have anorexia. I say "chose" because that is what she did. She ate what she wanted when her parents weren't watching. She was normal otherwise and we quickly became friends. Her parents had put her into the hospital to force her to eat, and she was very angry at them.

She said they controlled every aspect of her life, including financially, but her eating was one thing they couldn't control and she said it drove them crazy. No amount of money could fix this. She felt not eating gave her power. She was only there a few days, and they came to pick her up. I hugged her, noticing her tightly drawn mouth when her parents came into the room. We promised to write each other, but lost contact through the years.

I hated being in the hospital, but I was just trying to emotionally cope and stay alive for Heather's sake. My doctor's drug of choice for me toward the end of the five years of counseling was the benzodiazepine Xanax, after a trial of many different types of medication. I was on this medication for several years up until my last psychiatric voluntary hospitalization. Benzo drugs are addictive and can cause long-term physical, mental, and cognitive impairment.

Speaker/author Dana Arcuri writes in her memoir, *Harvest of Hope: Living Victoriously Through Adversity*, about her harrowing journey of drug dependency and toxic prescription interactions after being diagnosed with fibromyalgia, depression and anxiety. She was given prescriptions of Cymbalta, Ativan, and Prozac. While on the benzodiazepine Ativan, she attempted suicide through a drug overdose.

Afterward, realizing something was very wrong and that she

wasn't getting any better but worse, Dana insisted on being weaned off her medications. But her concerns were not taken seriously by her doctors. She went through what she calls "Ativan hell":

> Nationwide, there are men, women, and children suffering long-term debilitating consequences of benzodiazepines. Sadly, many have lost their jobs, families, marriages, homes, health, and their own lives. [102]

After Dana read the book *Addiction by Prescription: One Woman's Triumph and Fight for Change*, she was enraged.

> Suddenly, it occurred to me that I could have avoided my own hellish ordeal if Ativan wasn't prescribed in 2010. Silently, I thought, "If I knew then what I know now, I wouldn't have agreed to taking a mind-warping drug. If my doctor would have taken time to explain that Ativan may lead to physical dependence, I would have avoided it altogether.[103]

When she was no longer on Cymbalta, but prescribed Ativan, she expected to heal, but noticed a significant increase with anxiety, irritability, insomnia, and mood swings. Like a runaway train, her life was out of control; one minute she was screaming and throwing dishes across the room and the next she was sobbing and hibernating in her bedroom. Her family was afraid of her and avoided her.

"I was a train wreck!" Dana writes.[104]

Doing her own tiresome research about her debilitating symptoms, Dana decided to safely wean off Ativan. She discovered from credible sources that weaning off benzodiazepines was far worse than heroin. If a four-week Cymbalta taper led to her drug overdose, how could she manage an Ativan decrease alone since her doctor was away for one month from the office? He was on his honeymoon in the tropics and his nurse had told Dana she would have to taper Ativan without medical supervision.[105]

Eventually she had to enter the hospital to wean off it, because Dana felt her taper was going haywire and hurting her family. Benzos require a slow wean, but in the hospital she was given a "fast and furious taper"—which was very dangerous and potentially fatal.

Even after she was weaned off Ativan, she continued to experience anguish—symptoms ranging from extreme anxiety, agoraphobia, brain fog, blurry vision, crying spells, fear, fatigue, severe insomnia, irritability, panic attacks, and more.[106]

Looking back at all she and her family had been through, Dana cried for her lost years—missed opportunities to pursue her aspirations. "Drowning in sorrow, I cried for my family who stood by to observe my nightmare right along with me. They were forced to walk through the long, deep, muddy trenches with me."[107]

Taking back control of her mental, emotional, and physical health through faith in Christ, education, detoxing her body of prescriptions, chemicals, and unhealthy foods, and using exercise, essential oils, and Plexus products, today Dana is a picture of vibrant physical, emotional and spiritual health, although she has relapses occasionally from the fibromyalgia. She has learned much about triumphing over adversity, but paid it through a high price with her body and her mind.

I experienced those muddy trenches, too. While I didn't go through the toxic prescription interactions that Dana did, I did become physically dependent on Xanax and Ativan. I was in a hospital's drug rehab unit to detox from Ativan after my last psychiatric hospitalization. The hospital staff did a dangerously fast taper of the Ativan, which could have resulted in me having seizures or been fatal.

Shortly after my last traumatic hospitalization, I became pregnant with our daughter Leah and elected to wean off all medications to ensure her safety during my pregnancy. I was able to do a slow wean outside the hospital, with my doctor's careful supervision.

Thank God I got off Xanax, Ativan, and all medications over twenty years ago. God has done amazing, miraculous emotional, psychological, physical, and spiritual healing in my life and I am so grateful to Him. Halleluah! The only prescription medication I'm taking now is Ziac for stress-induced hypertension, which I pray one day I'll be able to get off of completely.

The world may promise healing through prescription medication (or even street drugs), therapists, psychiatrists, doctors, art therapy, counseling, and many other ways, but it always comes up empty. None of these things healed me. Jesus Christ healed me. He is the Jehovah Rophe, the Healer!

These are some of my most painful memories from the past—being emotionally unstable and often physically absent from Heather's life, during the times when I went into the hospital.

A memory that is especially painful for me was when Heather was "confirmed" at the Catholic church, where she attended parochial school up until seventh grade. I converted to Roman Catholicism in my early twenties and raised Heather as a Catholic, but we no longer attend the Catholic church.

Dressed in a pure white, lacey dress, white patent dress shoes, and an ornate veil, she walked down the aisle of the church for this important Catholic ordination ceremony, me her mother conspicuously absent, and my older brother having flown in from the south for the special occasion. I look at those pictures today of her sad face standing by my brother, and I cry. I wasn't there for her. God, have mercy.

I suppose it's not unlike drug or alcohol rehab, though. You are just trying to get better.

I'm so thankful that God has given me so many second chances in life, and that He has healed me from my painful past. I'm grateful that Heather has forgiven me, and that she and I are such close friends today. We talk every day and often see each other. She, her two beautiful girls Annabelle and Violet, my precious grandchildren, and my daughter Leah are such a joy to me.

## The Third Abortion

During that dark time in my life, as I worked through memories in counseling and during hospitalizations, I felt constantly afraid, sad, anxious, and very needy. During one of my hospitalizations, I met a Christian man, with whom I eventually became engaged—and I grew obsessed over him.

> *If you ever looked at me once with what I know is in you,*
> *I would be your slave.*
> *~ Emily Bronte ~*
> Wuthering Heights

After we were both discharged, we began dating and quickly became emotionally and sexually involved. It was as if he had become my everything and I couldn't breathe without him. But I was suffocating him. This man was the father of my third aborted child.

Both of us were in intense counseling sessions for our childhood sexual and physical abuse, and neither of us felt psychologically or financially prepared to have a child when I became pregnant. While this man didn't want me to have an abortion—he had plans to marry me soon and said he would love to have a child with me—he and I both felt that the timing was terribly wrong.

We were also worried how the stress of the pregnancy and the financial needs would affect me psychologically, with the childhood memories I was already trying to cope with and heal from in therapy. I was concerned the anti-depressant and anti-anxiety medications I had been on might have caused severe birth defects.

But I didn't want another abortion. With this pregnancy, I made a call to a pro-life pregnancy center to ask if they could help me. They couldn't provide monetary assistance with paying my rent and utilities, and they didn't have a place to offer me to stay with my child. Nor could they help with medical costs. They wanted to talk longer with me, but my primary need was financial help so I said, "No thank you," and hung up. Later this pregnancy center would be instrumental in my healing from Post Abortion Syndrome.

After talking many times with my fiancé and my therapist to make a decision about what to do, in much inner turmoil, I made an appointment at an abortion clinic. God tried to block my path from having this abortion.

On the paper that I had to fill out at the clinic, I was asked if I had any psychiatric history. When I wrote down "depression" and "anxiety disorder," the staff counselor said that I'd need a signed paper from my therapist and my psychiatrist in order to proceed with the abortion. This was to protect the clinic from any liability, should the abortion cause me any psychiatric problems. The clinic didn't want to be sued or held responsible for this.

I didn't realize that God in His Providence was trying to give me a chance to change my mind so my baby would live. Instead, I made an appointment with a different abortion clinic and didn't include my psychiatric history on it. I hid it. Secrets were becoming a way of life for me.

Evil thrives in darkness.

I knew by this time that abortion was morally wrong, so I was much more accountable to God for this abortion. I sensed that this baby was a little girl. Years later, I realized that not only had I lost three children through my abortions, but our daughters Heather, Eden, and Leah also lost three siblings with whom they could have grown up and loved.

God have mercy on me.

**Fear Was Driving My Life**

I was in so much fear that God was going to judge me for having this abortion (as well as my previous two), that after I was sent home from the abortion clinic to recover and I began bleeding profusely, I was convinced I was going to hemorrhage to death as punishment from God for my sin.

I called the clinic in a panic, and the doctor told me to come back into the clinic immediately. I couldn't find a babysitter. My fiancé and Heather went with me. I think Heather was about eight years old. To this day I will never know how deeply that affected Heather, and have had to forgive myself again and again for taking her there.

She didn't know I'd had an abortion. When we were driving to the clinic, I told her that I was going to a doctor "for a medical problem." At the clinic, she overheard the doctor talking to me and my fiancé and somehow surmised that I'd been pregnant. She asked in her innocent, sweet voice if I was going to have a baby. I went pale, and told her no.

After privately examining me, the abortion doctor said that apparently he "hadn't gotten all the tissue during the procedure." He told me that "this sometimes happens," and said that the heavy bleeding I'd been experiencing was probably my body "dispelling the rest of the tissue" at home. In other words, part of my baby went into the toilet.

Even writing these words makes me cringe inside. One of my best friends had a sudden miscarriage in the early weeks of her pregnancy at home and the nurse on the phone told her that the cramping, bleeding and clotting she had experienced in the bathroom was probably her body "dispelling tissue." My friend began sobbing into the phone and asked, "Are you telling me I just had my dead baby in the toilet?"

Aborted babies are disposed of in much worse ways at abortion clinics. Sometimes babies wind up in the trash when clinics cut costs and don't pay for disposal.[108]

**The Woman With the Issue of Blood**

I was so frightened when I began heavily bleeding at home that I was going to die and go to hell as punishment for this third abortion, and it took me years before I could release and be delivered from this fear of God's judgment and hell. The physical bleeding stopped at the clinic, but my soul kept bleeding the pain of shame and regret for years. Like the woman with the issue of blood, the only One who could miraculously heal me of my affliction was Jesus. I had to learn to reach out and touch the hem of His garment to become whole.

Did you know that people can be an idol, a false god? Anytime someone takes precedence in your thoughts over God, he or she becomes an idol. God is jealous for you with a fiery love and He will not permit you have to have any other gods before Him.

I was obsessed with the father of the baby. He had become my entire world and an idol. I wanted to hold him, breathe him in, possess him body and soul. My boundaries with him were very unhealthy, blurred as a Leonardo da Vinci sfumato' technique painting—I didn't know who was him and who was me.

I couldn't get enough of him, but he'd push me away, including sexually…while confessing that he had looked at pornography (*Playboy* and *Hustler* magazines) again at his friend's house. This caused me to feel angry and rejected and I'd verbally lash out at him. When he withdrew emotionally, I panicked, afraid of losing him, of losing myself.

My obsession with him and my intense jealousy of his female "friends" and even of his amazing art drove him away faster (drawing took him away from me and it made me feel like a failure, since I felt I had no obvious talents or writing success yet. He was an incredible artist.).

Our relationship began deteriorating rapidly after the abortion. Our counseling sessions were delving into more traumatic memories of our childhoods, the impact of the abortion, and our intense relationship difficulties. Neither of us was strong enough emotionally to help each other. In fact, our relationship was very sick.

We both had stopped working, and applied for disability income. We had too much time on our hands, when we weren't at counseling appointments and while Heather was at Catholic school during the daytime. We were consumed with guilt over the abortion, even though we felt it wasn't the right timing for a baby.

After one intense argument that we had, he made a serious suicide attempt and almost died. When I visited him in the hospital, his art therapist, an assigned member of his care team whom he had worked with before in a previous hospitalization, glared at me and walked angrily out of the room. She blamed me for this attempt. He refused to kiss me and I realized things were over between us.

We wanted our relationship to work out, but we were destroying each other.

> *I am getting nowhere with you and I can't let you go and I can't get through.*
> *~ Ani Difranco ~*

## Insatiable

Intense jealousy issues between us over friendships of the opposite sex and over his art, which took up a lot of his time, caused intense strife. I tried to focus on writing, but was locked up inside.

I was obsessed over him, and try as he might, he couldn't fill the enormous black hole inside of my soul. I was insatiable, and he couldn't give me the depths of love that I needed and that only God could provide.

He also was very needy, but didn't know exactly what he wanted.

One day we had an argument about his commitment to our relationship, with emotions spiraling out of control that resulted in a physical fight between us. All I remember after we started arguing is feeling his fist hit my face. I woke up seeing stars, stunned that he actually hit me—hard.

He was packing his belongings, with me crying and begging him not to leave. That day he moved out into his own place. He began withdrawing emotionally, and I panicked over losing him, which made him retreat further until he broke up with me.

I didn't think I'd be able to emotionally handle this breakup. But as Kelly Clarkson sings in her song *Stronger*, what doesn't kill you makes you stronger.[109] We are stronger than we believe! God was rescuing us both from a destructive, toxic relationship. Today I thank God we never married. It would have been a disaster.

**Obsession: Love in All the Wrong Places**

I saw him a couple of years later after I was married to Ray. He was out walking in my neighborhood. He'd seen a story in the local newspaper about Ray and me trying to renovate an old church near our apartment, to use it for ministry. He said he wanted to see the church. I think he really just wanted to see me, to make sure I was doing okay without him!

He was genuinely glad to see me and Heather and wished Ray and me the best. I realized that day what an enormous mistake it would've been to marry him. Our relationship was too messed up. We fed off each other's dysfunction. That day we apologized to each other and parted on friendly terms.

Through the years I have, as the cliché goes, looked for love in all the wrong places. All the relationships I've had with men were physically or verbally abusive. Many of them were not based on

God's biblical foundation, but on lust. I thought a man was the answer to my loneliness and my immense hurt inside. I thought a man could heal my brokenness.

*Promises in the dark.*

> *Before God could bring me to this place He has broken me a thousand times.*
> *~Smith Wigglesworth ~*

I also thought abortion would get rid of my "problems." My abortions compounded my pain. I deeply regret aborting these three precious babies and the sins I've committed in the past. I will never see these babies grow up, play, laugh, or fulfill the great purpose for which God created them. Yet I know I will see them in heaven and hold them one day.

## The Healing Balm of God's Forgiveness

Years later, I went through a post-abortion Bible study at the pro-life pregnancy center that I'd called for help with my third unexpected pregnancy. In this Bible study, I found out that God could and did forgive me for the three abortions. The revelation was shocking and humbling to me, and filled me with incredible joy.

For the first time in my life, I discovered God's unconditional love and forgiveness of my sins. I also learned to forgive myself, which was the hardest part, as it is for so many post-abortive women and men.

I didn't have to carry around this shame and burdensome, heavy weight any more. I didn't have to feel condemned any more for my mistakes or pay any kind of penance. Jesus paid the price in full for my sins and yours at Calvary over 2,000 years ago. He took our place to redeem us, so that we can live with God forever in Heaven.

Dear friend, if you've had an abortion, or more than one, please know that abortion is not the unforgiveable sin. All you have to do is come to Jesus, confess your sins accepting His completed work of redemption on the cross, and ask Him for forgiveness.[110]

Through this twelve-week Bible study, God broke the chains that held me in bondage for over six years. I was finally free from the shame and condemnation of my abortions. I no longer had to walk around feeling like a hypocrite as a Christian. I finally knew that I was forgiven. Though my sins were as scarlet, God washed them as white as snow.[111] After I went through the Bible study, the group leader, Annette Hopper, asked me to publicly speak in front of a group of leaders, sharing my testimony. I was terrified to speak, afraid of being judged, but I believe God told me to do it. My shackles of shame from the past were breaking. The audience was very gracious and encouraging.

Tears filled my group leader's eyes as I shared my story of liberating freedom. She knew that day I had taken a leap of faith and seized plunder from the enemy, Satan. Jesus Christ had been lifted up and glorified.

It was a life-changing moment of incredible victory, and the start of me stepping into my God-ordained purpose, using my spiritual gifts for God's glory.

> Strength and dignity are her clothing. And she smiles at the future.[112]

**180 Degrees**

As I began my post-abortion healing journey, God opened the door for me to volunteer at a pro-life pregnancy center to answer phones and to counsel pregnant girls and women. In counseling, I shared my testimony with other women who were considering abortion.

In two cases, my testimony caused the women to change their minds and have their babies. This filled me with so much joy. Two precious babies' lives were saved because of my story! God turned things around for me 180 degrees for His glory!

Three years ago, God opened the door for me to publicly share my testimony about my abortions and God's forgiveness at a women's Bible study, which officially began my speaking and writing career.

Many times after I've spoken at women's conferences and shared about my abuse, abortions, and other painful things in my past, women come forward for personal prayer and to confide in me, crying, that they have gone through this, too—and they've never told anyone! I'm able to pray with and minister to them God's healing, unconditional love and forgiveness to set them as captives free.

Through the powerful platform of the Internet and social media, God supernaturally began opening doors for me to also speak internationally in Haiti, the Bahamas, Canada, and Africa, sharing my testimony. God has used what Satan intended for evil for His purpose and glory. Isn't God amazing?

You can find out more about my women's conference keynote speaking at www.BethJones.net. I'd love to speak at your women's conference or event, or if you know of anyone who needs a speaker, please contact me at elizabethdjones@gmail.com.

The more I shared my story, the more my heart was healing—as well as other women's.

I was learning about God's grace and mercy. But like the character Much Afraid in Hannah Hurnard's book *Hinds' Feet On High Places*[113], I still had many more important lessons to learn. I thought that getting more education was the answer to my troubled life…and found out that this too is "meaningless. Completely meaningless!" (Ecclesiastes 1:2, NIV)

# Chapter 4

# education
# cinderella sweeping the floor

*"The beautiful thing about learning is that no one can take it away from you."*

~ B.B. King ~

My father was the son of a hard man, a poor tobacco and cotton crop farmer. My dad, his younger brother, and his younger sister worked hard every day in the field, from the time they were little until daddy was in his teens.

Inside their tiny white farmhouse, which is now dilapidated on their 80 acres in the country in south Georgia, my grandmother snapped beans, shucked corn, canned vegetables, and cooked, always offering buttered cornbread or some other type of homemade bread at supper.

My grandmother was a stern woman who wouldn't put up with any nonsense from her children or grandchildren, but she also had a good sense of humor and an infectious laugh. She had liquid, gentle brown eyes and black-grey hair that was waist long, but she kept it in a tight bun secured by bobby pins with a hair net over it, unless she was going out somewhere. Then she would put on a coal black, thick wig and a little lipstick.

She walked with a brown cane, had a green thumb that nobody could match to grow hearty plants and beautiful flowers in her yard, and knew how to squeeze pennies out of every dollar to save for a rainy day. She made the best pound cake and banana pudding I've ever eaten—and her warm, yellow cornbread was perfection.

While I was growing up, the nightly ritual was that my father would irritably ask my mother at supper time, "Where's the bread?" It's a mantra that I think of now as spiritual; Jesus is the bread of life.[114]

Mama would open the package of store-bought, bleached-white, Wonder Bread, and daddy would look at her in disgust out of the side of his eyes, but eat it anyway. Bread was a staple for meals. Daddy missed grandma's buttered cornbread. He didn't miss working in the crop field until dusk or his father's harshness.

I never knew my paternal grandfather; he died suddenly of a heart attack in his farm field, years before I was born.

Daddy had told us four kids a few stories about him after doing genealogy research. He was from generations of farmers. One exception was that one of the men generations back was a Methodist circuit rider preacher. This story fascinated and blessed me; I had the "preach" in my genes! That's where I got it from!

I felt I had missed out by being a "city girl" and not growing up on a farm in the country. Daddy thought differently. Animals, gardens, and tending and picking crops were a lot of work. Farm life was real hard, he said. He had to go to school in worn overalls and one year, he couldn't even afford shoes. I never knew if this part was true, but I've seen pictures of him as a child in the overalls.

## A Strong Work Ethic

Granddaddy was a small, thin man, uneducated, but was a hard worker and expected everyone else to be. He had a bad temper, my dad said; he cussed frequently and daddy feared him, having a couple of beatings by him for disobeying. He had little tolerance for laziness or disobedience.

Daddy inherited this trait, making us wake up early on Saturday mornings to rake leaves, vacuum, or wash our southern Victorian home's wrap-around, white-columned porch. "Sleeping in" or playing for long periods of time were unheard of in our family; idle hands were the devil's playground. Laziness was the worst sin you could have, in daddy's book.

At the time all of us kids resented this, but today I appreciate my father's hard work ethic and have inherited his workaholic tendencies. I never realized that entrepreneurship ran in my blood until this year, when I took a mastermind class and it dawned on me that I wanted to be a CEO and my own boss like my father—having my own successful home business like he did.

I'm now doing what I love, pursuing my passion. I'm able to enjoy my work on my laptop every day of being a Christian speaker, writer, and life coach. Two years ago, I began getting speaking invitations in other nations like the Bahamas, Canada, and my dream come true, Kenya, Africa.

Traveling is my passion and inspires my writing! When I'm on stage speaking to a live audience, I feel alive, happy, and energized. It is what God made me to do and to be. Work IS like play to me! You can find out more about my women's conference keynote speaking, writing, and coaching business at www.BethJones.net.

## Playing in the Office

As children, my siblings and I played "office" on nights when daddy was gone to town to get beer and peanuts to boil and eat while he watched Heehaw or Flip Wilson. I'd type on mama's electric typewriter or pretend to add up figures on the calculator, staple papers together (feeling so important!), file folders in the big, metal file cabinet, or make copies on the copy machine.

My cousin Cindy or my sister Maria would pretend to answer a ringing phone, and we loved calling each other on the intercom to let each other know that, "You have a call, ma'am."

Daddy had a small side room in his office filled with new office supplies of manila envelopes, crisp white and colored printer paper, and paper clips. This was a treasure chest of delightful riches for me. Who knew office supplies could be a girl's best friend? My online women entrepreneur friends today relate to playing "office" as children and make jokes about passionately shopping at Office Depot, Kinko's, and other office supply companies.

## Work as Identity

Our family's life centered around daddy's business since it was in our home. During office hours, mama would rush out into the hall with big eyes, saying, "SHHH! Your daddy has a client in the office!" after we got home from school, sliding down the stairs banister, and running wild through the house or fighting with each other. I never really knew what a "client" was, only some mysterious, faceless stranger meeting with daddy over business in the office and that he or she was ruining our fun!

But having the office in our home was financially advantageous to daddy on his taxes and he could spend time with his family whenever he wanted—or take off work to go play a round of golf at the country club with business peers and friends. It also meant that there was a very fine line separating family from work, and daddy's business and personal life. I remember as a child seeing daddy's shadowy figure with a dim light in the office late at night.

Sometimes he worked 10- or 12-hour days. He enjoyed his work. It fulfilled him. To this day he has a hard time not going into his office, working too much. He's now in his 70s. We kids are wondering if he will ever retire. I fear the day he does. Work is a large part of my father's identity. Will he feel lost, unhappy, or useless without it?

## No Poor Farmer

Getting a higher education and having a successful business has been an important achievement to my father. It separated him from the generations of poor farmers before him.

Daddy knew that he didn't want to be a farmer when he grew up. It was a hard life of relentless struggle, and often of abject poverty. Daddy didn't want this for his life. He was smart and loved learning. He had dreams of college and of a business career. Grandma wanted to make sure that daddy went to college. He was the first college graduate in his family and he worked hard to achieve his own successful business.

Daddy's younger brother quickly followed daddy's example, getting his college degree and working for daddy part-time in his business when he wasn't in the hospital. My uncle's life was plagued with medical problems. He was born with a genetic hip defect that required painful back surgery and caused him to limp when he walked. He was a smoker and was eventually diagnosed with lung cancer, undergoing chemotherapy and years of painful suffering. He was put on a long list of hopeful patients for a heart-lung transplant, until his death in his late 30s. Despite his trials, he always had a positive outlook.

Working for daddy was a gift of grace for him and fun for us kids.

My uncle grew up in the hippy '60s, a different generation than my father's. When he stopped working for daddy to pursue his passion of music, he grew out his hair long and played the guitar in bars. He would often say "groovy" and "cool."

Uncle had a sanguine personality. He loved life, Jesus, and to have fun. He laughed a lot and made us kids giggle. His laugh was a sudden, loud burst of happiness, a deep, hearty, genuine laugh, which was a stark contrast to our father's stern, serious, melancholy personality. Daddy rarely cracked a smile, but when he laughed, it was a freeing laugh like a river that made me smile with great joy. I've always felt like daddy should laugh more. I've inherited this trait of being too serious; thank God for my kids who laugh a lot and remind me that you shouldn't take life, or yourself, so seriously. Uncle would hug us kids tight and ask us who our favorite uncle was while tickling us.

He bought a camera and often took pictures of people, especially our family. This is one thing he and I had in common.

His first love was always music, and he played the electric guitar in a band until he died. While their personalities were very different, he always looked up to daddy and deeply respected him, especially for his education and his career success.

## Business Is in Our Blood

My mother earned a B.A. in business. She majored in psychology to become a psychologist until daddy convinced her to change her major to business to help him. She was daddy's secretary until she died at forty-two years old of health complications. Daddy has hired a lot of help through the years, but says no woman has ever come close to matching mama's intelligence and skillful help in his business.

I've often wondered if mama ever regretted surrendering her dreams of being a psychologist to help my dad. My older brother followed daddy's footsteps in his career, working for daddy until he joined a larger firm in northern Georgia, where he still lives. He may take over daddy's business one day, unless daddy sells it.

My sister Maria worked for daddy for a long time, too. Two years ago, she graduated with her B.A. degree in psychology, having made dean's list every semester her last year of college, while working part-time and being a single mom, taking care of her three children! She just graduated from college with a master's degree in psychology. She has registered for the state test to be licensed as a therapist and just got a job working in her career field.

My younger brother graduated from college with a business degree and has worked primarily in management positions.

I have an executive secretarial degree from Valdosta Vocational Training School, three years of college studies with hopes to complete my B.A. degree one day, and earned a B.A. in Christian Psychology from Jacksonville Theological Seminary in Jacksonville, FL. I now operate my own speaking business/ministry at www.BethJones.net. Education and business are in our family's blood.

One day I hope to finish secular college for a four-year degree. (I don't like anything that is unfinished.)

It all started with my father being the first college graduate of his family. Like daddy, I love education and learning. I believe that we should learn something new every day for our whole lives.

I'm continually taking online classes and courses to grow in knowledge and further my training– speaking and writing classes, business webinars, telecalls, and mastermind classes. I also attend professional speakers' live training events for continuing education.

## The Alluring Promises of Higher Education

Daddy is proud of what he achieved coming from his humble beginnings (and should be!) and wants all of us to have college educations. As kids we grew up hearing the constant adage, "Nobody can ever take away your education."

Our father pushed us hard academically in school. He said we needed to study every day and to make the best grades possible. A good report card resulted in being rewarded with cash, to our delight. Failing classes resulted in our punishment; even making B's or C's in classes were unacceptable to him. He expected more from his children because all his children were smart, he said. All you had to do to make good grades was to study. He was living proof. I've always respected my father for his sharp intelligence, his hard work, and his business acumen and success. But the man is a perfectionist! (It's where I get mine from!)

I remember one time I brought home a report card with an "A" in a class in which I'd been struggling. Daddy looked at it and asked, "Why didn't you make an A+?" I've struggled with perfectionism my entire life, remembering in the back of my mind that moment, the daddy thought that I can push myself harder, I can make that perfect A+. *Good isn't good enough.* For my father, an "A" wasn't enough when you could make a higher grade. He believed earning top grades got you further in life and were a fine achievement. To him, top A's are a promise of "the good life"—of success. The world promises you much through education.

Excelling in school had given my father his dreams of a college education and being a successful businessman.

> *What sculpture is to a block of marble, education is to the human soul.*
> *~ Joseph Addison ~*

**Education As a God**

Daddy is in his seventies and is just now thinking about retirement. His physical health has been failing the last several years, which is heart-breaking to me. He has told me that he desires "quality of life" physically in his old age, but his mind and continual learning are more important to him than his bodily health.

Despite the dysfunctional events that happened in my childhood, I don't ever want anything to happen to my family. I want daddy to live to a ripe, old age. I absolutely dread the day my sister calls me from Georgia to tell me that daddy has passed away; it freaks me out to even think about it. I've had a lot of dreams about it, which I feel is just God preparing me for when it really does happen. But maybe we'll get lucky and the rapture will occur first. I dearly love my father.

My dad still drives and travels, driving to the mountains in north Georgia once or twice a year with his companion of twenty-five years. (He began dating her a year after mama died, and they've been together ever since.) He reads the newspaper daily and fusses at my sister Maria for not keeping up with current events. He reads other books and resources, watches the news on TV, and stays alert mentally.

When my sister Maria graduated this past year from college, my father told her three or four times how proud he was of her. Education is very important to my father.

But is education my father's salvation and god? Is it yours? At times it has been mine. I've believed the lie that furthering my education and excelling in studies would validate me, would affirm my worth. I thought that it would earn my father's approval, and other people's. That somehow it would make my life matter and have more significance.

I know that education helped to make my father's dreams come true and it can help your dreams, too. But no matter how much or little education you have, you are precious and valuable to God.

## Higher Education Doesn't Increase Your Value as a Person

My intrinsic worth—and yours—only comes from an intimate relationship with God. In Him we live and move and have our being.[115] We have been bought at a price, and aren't to be slaves to any man or the world.[116]

Education is a great thing. God wants us to learn new things every day and to grow in knowledge. I love traveling, meeting new people, seeing new things, and trying new foods. I read constantly.

I'm never without a stack of new books to read at night.

I love learning something new every day and I'm constantly attending business training webinars, teleseminars, conferences, and workshops. I also am in a mastermind group with my speaking coach and another woman in an online business.

This year I joined a group of women for speaker/author Donna Partow's 90-Day Renewal for the Spirit, Soul, and Body called *The Ultimate Year*, which includes prayer calls, videos and teleseminars, coaching on live calls and in our private Facebook forum, and accountability to each other for our daily, continual progress.

I believe it's very important to keep our minds alert and sharp and to fulfill our greatest potential. We need to use and improve our spiritual gifts for God's glory, honing our skills and talents, and increasing our knowledge and education. We leave far too much of our brain's power untapped.

> Let the wise hear and increase in learning, and the one who understands obtain guidance.[117]

But education is never to be our god. It doesn't add one cent to our value and intrinsic worth. God loves us unconditionally. He created us wonderfully and fearfully in our mother's womb.[118] Her stepmother and stepsisters thought Cinderella was only good for sweeping the floor, but she was destined for greatness, and so are you.

God saw all the days of our lives before we were even born, and His thoughts toward us are precious and outnumber the grains of sand on a beach.[119]

## God Loves Us All the Same

If we never went to school or college a day in our life or learned anything new, God would love us just as much. God doesn't love us based on our knowledge or education. He doesn't rank a person with a doctorate degree more valuable than, say, an "ignorant hillbilly" in the mountains of Kentucky. God loves all of us the same and warns us as His children not to show favoritism.

> If you really keep the royal law found in Scripture, "Love your neighbor as yourself," you are doing right. But if you show favoritism, you sin and are convicted by the law as lawbreakers.[120]

While higher education may offer advantages in ministry, job, career, political, or military opportunities, it doesn't increase our worth or significance.

Maybe you never made it past eighth grade or had to drop out of high school or college. My paternal grandmother had only a seventh-grade education. Yet when her husband died, leaving her a widow and single mother in her thirties, she raised her three children successfully, kept a roof over their heads, and died in her nineties, having lived a full life.

She was never wealthy by the world's standards, but was rich in devotion to family and friends. She loved her family, sewed beautiful quilts, was a talented cook, made the most delicious desserts, and left a legacy of love and loyalty to family. She was an excellent listener (something I could learn from!) and often encouraged others. She was also a very generous woman, despite her limited financial resources. She encouraged us to further our education and to do our best in life.

## You Have Great Value

Maybe you struggle with feelings of shame or unworthiness because you don't have a higher education like others. Maybe you've always wanted to graduate from high school or college, and never had the opportunity and you've always felt "less than"—not good enough.

I want to encourage you, dear friend, that you are enough! God loves you and you don't need to feel ashamed or embarrassed about your education. You are of great value in His sight—so precious that Jesus Christ laid down His life for you to save you and have an eternal relationship with you!

> I came so that everyone would have life, and have it in its fullest.[121]

Yes, getting education or learning *is* a good thing! *But it does not define you and it can't save you*. Higher education may promise you "the world." But you are "the world" to God! He can give you what no education, training or college degree can offer: eternal life.

Here's another one of God's precious promises for you:

> Are not two sparrows sold for a cent? And yet not one of them will fall to the ground apart from your Father. But the very hairs of your head are all numbered. So do not fear; you are more valuable than many sparrows.[122]

Of course, if you really want to get more education or learn new things, pray and ask God to help you. It's never too late to learn new things, even if you're a senior citizen! An ordinary farmer's wife and mother of five children, Grandma Moses began painting folk art in her late 70s—and her painting *Sugaring Off* sold in

November 2006 for $1.2 million! Now that's the way to retire!

But know that, "Fear of the LORD is the foundation of true wisdom. All who obey his commandments will grow in wisdom."[123]

Education is not the only place where we can try to seek our identity and affirmation. We can also put false hopes in other things—or in other people, even ones who don't belong to us.

# Chapter 5

# adultery
# other dreams

*"I tried to keep myself away from him by using con words like 'fidelity' and 'adultery,' by telling myself that he would interfere with my work, that if I had him I'd be too happy to write. I tried to tell myself I was hurting Bennett, hurting myself, making a spectacle of myself. I was. But nothing helped. I was possessed. The minute he walked into a room and smiled at me, I was a goner."*

*- Erica Jong,* Fear of Flying~

I married my first husband, Kevin,[124] my high school sweetheart, in my senior year of high school. No, I wasn't pregnant. We hadn't even had sex yet. But my father was very strict and I desperately wanted to get out of the house from underneath his control…and Kevin and I thought we wanted to be together "all the time." Truly love is blind!

Kevin and I knew nothing about marriage or covenant. We were just two selfish, immature kids who thought we were in love. The honeymoon phase quickly ended with the startling realization of adult responsibilities like full time work, college classes, bills, and what a successful marriage really involves—self-denial, understanding and agape love.

We desperately struggled on Kevin's assistant manager pay to take care of the monthly apartment rent, the electric bill and groceries, and fought like cats and dogs over stupid things like the toilet seat being up. To cope with shattered expectations and stress, we partied on the weekends with friends, drinking beer and eating pepperoni pizza. Most of the time, there was more month than money!

One weekend, drinking too much and bored out of my mind as I watched Kevin play a poker card game with his beer buddies, I noticed Kevin's sister's boyfriend Todd[125] looking discreetly with interest at me. I playfully winked at him. He looked like he was going to fall over from shock. Then he winked back; he said later this was to test me to see if I'd really winked at him on purpose. It became a childish, absurd game with us winking at each other the rest of the night.

Several days later, Kevin, Todd and I ran an errand in town together. Todd deliberately tagged along to try to talk to me. As Kevin went into the store alone to get what he needed, Todd asked me why I'd winked at him at the party. I laughed loudly and uncomfortably, and he asked again, a little hurt at my response.

I was embarrassed and turned red-faced, mumbling something inane. Todd reached over the front seat to hold my hand. His hand was cold and clammy; it oddly reminded me of a reptile's claw. He looked at me with passionate fire in his eyes. The attention, though none other than lust, was flattering. We made plans then to see each other that week and soon were involved in a full-blown, physical affair.

Months later, Kevin's sister found a note in his jeans pocket in the dirty laundry that I'd written Todd and she confronted him. She was shocked that it was me, because I was a "usually moral person." When he told her the truth, she told her mother and Kevin, bawling. Kevin cried loudly, too.

His sobs reminded me of an animal wail, and I realized how deeply I'd wounded him. I remember with shame seeing Kevin's sister look at me with such hurt and betrayal, her Joan Jett-like, thick, black eyeliner and liquid mascara running down her freckled face. I felt horrible for hurting everyone the way I did. The affair ended that night, stopping as suddenly as it began.

Years later after my divorce, Todd and I began dating. It was another big mistake. I began to feel suffocated from his jealous obsession over me and tried to think of a way to end things between us. That ending was through an abortion. Todd became the father of my first aborted baby. He wanted to keep the baby, but I was adamant.

To this day, I'm not really sure why I had the affair or the ones for years after it. I do know the fruit of adultery is rotten. Adultery makes you feel guilty, condemned, and fearful. You're always afraid you're going to get caught. Some people think the secrecy is what adds to the "excitement" of it, but some men and women have injured or killed an adulterous spouse and/or their lover. There's nothing cute about it. Adultery robs you of peace, and it shatters lives.

The Bible says in Proverbs 5:3-11, The Message: "The lips of a seductive woman are oh so sweet, her soft words are oh so smooth. But it won't be long before she's gravel in your mouth, a pain in your gut, a wound in your heart. She's dancing down the primrose path to Death; she's headed straight for Hell and taking you with her. She hasn't a clue about Real Life, about who she is or where she's going....You don't want to squander your wonderful life among the hardened. Why should you allow strangers to take advantage of you?...You don't want to end your life full of regrets, nothing but sin and bones."

## A Vessel of Brokenness

> *God whispers to us in our pleasures, speaks in our conscience, but shouts in our pains: it is His megaphone to rouse a deaf world.*
> ~ C. S. Lewis ~

I've committed adultery several times in my life and learned firsthand its destructiveness. Both my ex-husbands committed adultery, so I'm also well aware of the piercing, horrible pain of its betrayal and how it devastates lives. It is a completely selfish act.

Yet God's eye is on the sparrow that falls to the ground.[126] He, the Potter, knows that we are made of dust; we are but fragile, imperfect clay. When the Potter sees that the clay is marred and good for nothing, He begins making it into a new vessel that seems good to Him to make.[127]

As only God can do, He now uses me as a clay vessel of brokenness to minister to and help other hurting women who have been through abuse, abortion, and adultery—and other painful situations. (You can find out more about my keynote speaking, products, and coaching services at http://www.bethjones.net.)

Many people who commit adultery have deep wounds from childhood. This doesn't excuse adultery, but it helps to understand the "why" behind the actions. Men and women who were abused as children are more vulnerable to adultery, as well as being preyed on, like I was when I was a patient in the hospital. Predators look for weak people. Having been abused as a child—especially having been sexually abused—makes one vulnerable to being revictimized.[128]

A research study done by the Maine Department of Behavioral and Developmental Services (Office of Trauma Services) showed that women who are sexually abused during childhood were 2.4 times more likely to be revictimized as adults as women who were not sexually abused.[129]

Twice as many women with a history of incest as women without such a history are victims of domestic violence, and twice as many also report unwanted sexual advances by an unrelated authority figure.[130]

Many women who have been victimized in childhood are preyed upon as adults. They are given promises in exchange for their bodies. This is what happened to me. The psychiatric technician at the hospital constantly told me how beautiful I was and said he wanted to marry me.

I didn't seriously consider the technician's proposal, but my ego longed to hear those words, "You are beautiful." Every woman wants to hear those words from a man. Every man wants his woman to admire and respect him. This is human nature and the way God wired us.

> We think that you'll find every woman in her heart of hearts longs for three things: to be romanced, to play an irreplaceable role in a great adventure, and to unveil beauty. That's what makes a woman come alive.[131]

Adultery offers the promise of unconditional love and a fantasy of "happily-ever-after" romance. But like the poison apple that Sleeping Beauty ate, Satan's promises are lies and are fatal.

> Mark well that God doesn't miss a move you make; He's aware of every step you take. The shadow of your sin

will overtake you; you'll find yourself stumbling all over yourself. Death is the reward of an undisciplined life.[132]

**Anything for Love**

A man craves respect, and a woman desires love. Sometimes girls or women will do anything for love, including giving a boy or a man (or even another woman) sex in exchange for love. Sometimes men will do anything for respect and admiration. That anything can include adultery. In the story of Cinderella, I wonder if the Prince had stopped dancing with her after marriage, would she have sought "other dreams?"

Every woman wants to hear the words, "You are beautiful," and "I love you."

Missy was a September 18, 2013 guest on Dr. Phil's show *Dangerous Online Obsession*. She is a seventeen-year-old girl, whose mother Mary says has a dangerous addiction to the Internet.

She has met and had sex with many men whom she's met online — Mary says anywhere from twenty to twenty-five men, and Missy claims over a hundred — who have traveled to see her, some from "great distances," her mom Mary says.

Missy, like many women, is desperate to feel loved and to feel beautiful.[133]

This desire to feel beautiful includes married women (even Christian married women).

According to Peggy Vaughan, author of *The Monogamy Myth*, conservative estimates are that 60 percent of men and 40 percent of women will have an extramarital affair.[134] This assessment was made over a decade ago, so it's probably even more prevalent today.

The increase of women in the workplace and on the Internet likely means that the number for women having extramarital affairs has increased to at least 60 percent, too. In fact, Vaughan's book's premise is that monogamy is a myth and not the norm.

## But Why?

No one is immune to an affair. Why? Because we're all human and it promises happiness and satisfaction.

Below are reasons cited for extramarital affairs:

- Attraction—sex, companionship, admiration, power
- Novelty
- Excitement, thrill, risk, or challenge
- Curiosity
- Enhanced self-image
- Falling in love
- Desire to escape from a painful relationship
- Boredom
- Desire to fill gaps in relationship
- Desire to punish a partner
- Need to prove attractiveness or worth
- Desire for attention
- Societal factors—affairs are glamorized in movies, news, politics, novels, advertising.

None of these reasons justify adultery, but it can help us to understand why people have affairs. I don't think anyone plans to have an affair. Many times, the affair takes even the person involved by surprise. It's usually a gradual descent into darkness and deception, one small compromise after another, until it's too late. Afterward, he or she is filled with a sickening feeling of guilt and deep remorse. Only the blood of Jesus can erase this guilt. Only God can heal and restore you—and your spouse—after adultery.

I have a friend who slept with a married woman after his wife of twenty-one years tragically died in an accident. He was just lonely and hurting. He was close friends with both the husband and the wife, and could hardly look either of them in the eye after this one-time sexual incident happened. He buried himself in his work and in activities with his kids to avoid seeing the couple socially any more. Filled with shame, he cried as he confessed his sin of adultery to Ray and me. The husband still doesn't know about the betrayal.

Another friend of Ray's and mine began a "sexting" relationship with a woman on his smart phone, when he was already engaged to a woman he loved. One night when he went to work, he forgot his phone and his fiancé discovered the inappropriate texts when she looked at his phone. She called him at his workplace and angrily confronted him: "What the he---?!"

He still doesn't know why he did this, but it wreaked havoc in the relationship with his fiancé. The "sexting" caused a wall of distrust and suspicion, and filled him with shame and guilt. If they do marry, the enemy Satan is sure to use this as a wedge between them and as a weapon in arguments later to create strife and unforgiveness.

Another long-married couple friend of ours had their marriage vows tested when the wife had an emotional affair with a former boyfriend. The husband found the texts on her phone and confronted her.

She 'fessed up, stopped the affair immediately, and repented to
God and her husband, but lost her women's ministry job as a result
of her indiscretion and unfaithfulness. Christians in ministry aren't
immune to adultery. And there are consequences to our actions.

Adultery, whether it is a physical or emotional affair, pornography,
Internet chat room flirting, phone "sexting," or mental fantasy
causes great pain to the person who is betrayed. It's almost
unbearable emotionally. I believe that very few married couples
can stand and truly heal from adultery, in whatever form it takes.
It's like two battering rams that won't stop fighting to the death.
Forgiveness in this situation is so hard. Please think before you do
this, breaking your spouse's heart and potentially destroying yours,
your spouse's, and your children's lives. I have experienced its
devastation, from both sides of the coin.

## God Understands the Pain of Adultery

God understands the pain of adultery and faithlessness. He was so
hurt by Israel's idolatry that He divorced her. He speaks about his
beloved's adultery in Jeremiah 3:8 NLT and gives her a certificate of
divorce:

> She saw that I divorced faithless Israel because of her
> adultery. But that treacherous sister Judah had no fear, and
> now she, too, has left me and given herself to prostitution.

Basically God was saying His people were acting like a "ho."
(Remembering the movie, *Sleepless In Seattle*, when the young
son Jonah is upset when he sees his widowed dad, Sam, kissing a
female co-worker he's dating, Victoria, outside on the deck. "She's
a ho!" Jonah yells into the phone with the talk radio show host
in protest, whom he called at Christmas to talk about missing his

deceased mom. If you haven't seen it, it's a great movie![135])

God's been there. His beloved is acting the part of a "ho." God knows what unfaithfulness feels like. The pain. The betrayal. The anger. I don't think there is any pain like it.

God sees all the tears you have cried:

> You have seen how many places I have gone. Put my tears in your bottle. Are they not in Your book. Then those who hate me will turn back when I call. I know that God is for me. I praise the Word of God. I praise the Word of the Lord. In God I have put my trust.[136]

Adultery promises you happiness, fulfillment, great sex, a renewed sense of self-worth and self-esteem, excitement, youthfulness, adventure, fun, and so much more. For a little while it may bring you these things, but the rewards are fleeting and leave you empty. Adultery is one of the most selfish things you can ever do. Its consequences are destructive and deadly. It's a dead end.

> For the lips of an immoral woman are as sweet as honey, and her mouth is smoother than oil. But in the end she is as bitter as poison, as dangerous as a double-edged sword. Her feet go down to death; her steps lead straight to the grave.[137]

Adultery promises so much…and delivers nothing but destroyed lives.

## The Woman with the Scarlet Letter

I confess that I had several adulterous relationships with men in my first marriage (my then-husband also had sex with 3 other women while we were married, but that doesn't justify what I did). I wish I'd never done this, hurting God, my ex-husband, myself and others so much. Afterward, I felt like Hester in the book *The Scarlet Letter* by Nathaniel Hawthorne, branded with a scarlet letter A on my chest.

Some of my adulterous affairs happened for only one night and I never saw the man again. Others lasted weeks or months. One affair I had was with an attorney I'd consulted for my first divorce. I didn't hire him. But he called me after the consult to ask me to dinner. I was young, pretty, and back then very seductive. Yes, I was hurting. Very scared. Lonely. Vulnerable. He was much older than me, and his attention was flattering, a balm to my wounded soul after the collapse of my marriage. "Catching" someone so wealthy and prominent was like a "prize." I was with a rich attorney, someone who had a black Jag!

After we slept together at one of the multiple houses he owned, he offered to put me up in an apartment that he would pay for (I was living at my dad's house at the time, and he didn't want to come pick me up there!). In other words, be his mistress.

I was flattered (what?!), but deep inside I knew it was wrong. I hedged and said I had to think about it.

Soon after that, I ended the affair when I met a man my age (who was not married!). When I told the attorney that I wanted things to end, he asked if there was someone else and I said yes.

"Ahh," he said in his sophisticated manner. "I've been dumped for someone younger." His attorney big ego was bruised.

I don't know why I did this. I could say that I was just young and stupid, but let's call a spade a spade, shall we? The only way we'll ever get healed, delivered, and set free is if we will just admit that what we've done is wrong. God plainly calls it "sin."

> Make this your common practice. Confess your sins to each other and pray for each other so that you can live together whole and healed.[138]

I deeply regret doing what I've done in the past, but am so thankful that God can and does forgive the sin of adultery.

How did I meet these men with whom I had affairs? Different ways. Some at work, even my bosses.

Statistics show that 46 percent of unfaithful wives and 65 percent of unfaithful husbands have had affairs with someone at work. It usually starts out as friendship, with the spouse feeling like the co-worker understands him or her much better than his/her spouse does. Other statistics are that 80 percent of men and women have fantasies about co-workers.[139]

Each of the men I committed adultery with were different types of personalities, different ages, different faiths or religions, and/or different social and economic backgrounds.

No one is immune to committing adultery. No one is invincible or above it. In fact, the Bible warns that if you're walking in pride and thinking you'd never do this, that you're incapable of sinning, standing strong, you may fall.[140] Anyone can become entangled in the deception of an affair; its devastating results are the same for everyone.

This is why the Bible warns us, "He who commits adultery lacks sense; he who does it destroys himself."[141]

Today I look back at my life and wonder how could I have done this? It sounds cliché and like a cop-out, but it's so true: I was looking for love in all the wrong places. I was looking for **authentic love**. I never found it in adultery and I hurt God and devastated many people's lives in the process. Only God can give us that unconditional, agape, authentic love that we are desperately seeking.

Learn my hard lessons well. Can I tell you that the guilt from adultery will eat you alive? It robs you of intimacy with God and your spouse, and steals sweet sleep, peace, and joy. It consumes your life and fills you with shame.

I've battled a lot of fear sharing about this topic of adultery with you. In fact, a friend questioned me writing about the adultery because it might hurt those I love. It probably will hurt them. It's hurt me, too. The writing of this book has left my soul feeling raw, out in the open, like a wounded gazelle that can't keep up with the herd that a lioness has targeted for the kill.

No, I didn't want to write this book. I've written six books and struggled with major resistance to writing this one. It's taken me over a year to do it. This book is the most vulnerable book I've ever written. I'm exposing myself, laying myself bare for the whole world to see my shameful nakedness, my sins, my dirt. There's no fig leaf to cover me, nowhere to run and hide. I'm sharing with you my rock bottom moments.

> Always wondering if we're good enough, pretty enough, smart enough. We're not-so-secret wrecks. We all know it, but we don't talk about it. Instead, we grab the mask that hides what we lack. And if that mask doesn't work, we mask our masks.[142]

But it's time to pull off my mask—and yours. If this book can help just one woman to avoid my big mistakes and sins that grieved God, if it can help just one person realize that Jesus Christ is the answer to life's troubles, then I have done my job and my mission is accomplished!

If this book can help you to finally see and know, sweet friend, that God will forgive you of any wrong you have done, then my work here isn't in vain. It will be worth it all. God's arms are open wide for you; His love and His forgiveness are unconditional and limitless. His promises are true and faithful.

This book may also serve as a warning to you. Maybe you are thinking, "I don't want to end my affair (or porn, or mental fantasy, or emotional affair)! I'm happy for once!"

The truth is that *illicit sex feels good*. If it didn't feel good, you wouldn't be doing it! Right?

And yes for awhile, you might feel happy. We can't live our lives by feelings or we will run smack-dab into a royal mess. I know a Christian woman who was a paramedic, who left her husband and their young children to have an affair with a hot, wealthy doctor at work. She told my husband that she'd never been so happy in her life. She wound up divorcing her husband, breaking his heart, and marrying the other man. Her Christian testimony is now ruined and her ex-husband's life is devastated from her selfish choices.

And what's worse is how this has affected their children, who are confused, sad, hurt, and angry. Their lives will never be the same again. Oh God, the children! Why don't we ever think of what it will do the kids, how it will screw up their lives?

This life is not just about me—or you! Our actions have a deep and lasting impact on other people, and on generations to come.

> I am slow to anger, and filled with unfailing love and faithfulness. I lavish unfailing love to a thousand generations. I forgive iniquity, rebellion, and sin. But I do not excuse the guilty. I lay the sins of the parents upon their children and grandchildren; the entire family is affected — even children in the third and fourth generations.[143]

I don't want to cause more problems in my kids' lives, or their kids' and future generations, do you? Life is hard enough as it is.

## We're Called to Be Holy

But we're a selfish people. We want to "just be happy." You know, like the cute little song in *The Lion King* movie, *Hakuna Matata*[144] (which means, no worries for the rest of your days). Can I tell it like it is, at the risk of offending you? God hasn't called you and me to be happy, but to *be holy because He is holy*.[145]

No matter how much you try to tell yourself in this affair that you are finally happy, you know deep inside *it is terribly wrong*. Its consequences are severe and irreparable.

There were many men I've met along life's journey who I knew I *could* have had an affair with, because of the way they flirted with and came onto me. A woman can tell when a man is attracted to her or is interested in her sexually; a man can tell when a woman is, too.

*Watch out! Be alert! The opportunity for adultery is always there.*

So be careful. If you are thinking, "Oh, I would never behave like that"—let this be a warning to you. For you too may fall into sin.[146]

Maybe this is you. You're about to jump off the cliff. You're feeling tempted by that man or woman at work, church, online, or wherever. You think maybe your marriage was a mistake and this is really "the one."

Maybe God even brought this person into your life for you to divorce your spouse and marry! (Yes, I've heard this excuse!) Friend, you're being deceived!

Your feelings are already engaged. You've never felt this way before! How can this be so wrong if it feels so right, right? Wrong! Satan is baiting you.

Your lust is out of control now. Maybe just one kiss wouldn't hurt. Or a hug. Or a glass of wine or coffee together.

Don't do it! Run, like Joseph did![147]

Or maybe you've already had a secret affair. No one knows but you and God. It's eating you alive. You're filled with shame and regret. You feel guilty all the time and you can hardly look your spouse in the eye. You feel like a hypocrite at church.

Don't despair. If you've committed adultery, God will forgive you. Come to Him. Ask forgiveness and repent.

Of course, break all ties with the person you are involved with now. It will be impossible for you to stop having an affair if you continue seeing him or her, calling, texting, emailing, or somehow keeping in contact with that person. If you work together, you need to pray fervently about finding a new job!

Ask your spouse's forgiveness and go to Christian marriage counseling. It's going to be an upward climb and you'll want to quit many times. It might take years for your marriage to be restored. Your relationship has been violently ripped apart. But it's necessary to get the help you need and do the inside-out work to heal.

If your spouse is willing to reconcile, rebuild your marriage and your lives. Sometimes this isn't possible if your spouse won't choose to forgive or you won't forgive him or her for your spouse's affair. Sometimes it just feels impossible because of the enormous pain and distrust it causes. But nothing is impossible with God.[148] God is a miracle working God!

**God Will Restore What Was Stolen From You**

An affair is one of the most painful things a married couple could go through. But God promises to heal and restore you. It's not easy. It takes forgiveness, hard work, counseling, and day-by-day restoration of trust. But with God, you can get through it and your marriage can be healed and restored.

If you have experienced the devastating pain of adultery (either your spouse had a physical or emotional affair or you did), meditate on these comforting promises from God:

> So I will restore to you the years that the swarming locust has eaten, the crawling locust, the consuming locust, and the chewing locus, My great army which I sent among you. You shall eat in plenty and be satisfied, and praise the name of the Lord your God who has dealt wonderously with you; And My people shall never be put to shame. Then you shall know that I am in the midst of Israel; I am the Lord your God and there is no other. (Joel 2:25-27, NKJV)

> I'm going to give you a new heart, and going to give you a new spirit within all of your deepest parts. I'll remove that rock-hard heart of yours and replace it with one that's sensitive to me. (Joel 36:26, ISV)
>
> But did He not make them one, having a remnant of the Spirit? And why one? He seeks godly offspring. Therefore take heed to your spirit, and let none deal treacherously with the wife of his youth. "For the Lord God of Israel says that He hates divorce, for it covers one's garment with violence," says the Lord of hosts. "Therefore take heed to your spirit, that you do not deal treacherously." (Malachi 2:15-16, NKJV)

God can heal your marriage. He can make it brand new through the same resurrection power He used to raise Christ from the dead.

With God there's always hope.

# Chapter 6

# marriage
# dancing with the prince

*"Marriage is the only war in which you sleep with the enemy."*
*~ Anonymous ~*

Marriage is definitely not a subject on which I feel qualified to write! I've been through two divorces and this marriage has been hell!

Yet marriage is another one of the ways I've sought to find authentic love. It has eluded me for my entire life.

Marriage, for many people, is the ultimate promise of "happily ever after." Author Alisa Bowman writes in her book, *Project: Happily Ever After*[149], about how she and her husband Mark began bickering over every little thing:

- he wanted the bathroom counters cleared of clutter, she didn't;
- he didn't think she washed clothes correctly; she accused him of shrinking her favorite sweater and he blamed it on the cleaning lady.

When they weren't fighting, they had nothing to say. They'd go to dinner and stare at their food, "the silence between us as thick as our butternut squash soup. I began to hate when he was home. His eyes were so cold and his jaw so set. I assumed he resented me. I believed that, in talking him into becoming a father, I had ruined his life."

Meanwhile, Alisa was excelling in her career, exercising, and noticing other men looking at her. She thought marrying Mark was a mistake.

They had nothing in common. So when she met Deb in New York, she was 15,000 words into the story of how she would eventually kill her husband. Deb had made her promise to work on her marriage. One night at the grocery store, Alisa got so mad at Mark that she decided to write a novel about how she would kill him. She told Deb about this.

> "Oh my God, that's great. You're writing a novel? That's great! Tell me more."
>
> "It's about this naïve girl who gets knocked up by a player, marries him, and then eventually finds herself stuck in a terrible marriage. She doesn't want to divorce him. I'm not sure why…I still have to figure out why divorce isn't an option. Anyway, she decides to kill him."
>
> "How does she kill him?"
>
> "I don't know. I'm stuck on that because I want her to get away with it. Maybe she poisons him." She and Deb decide that was too cliché. Maybe he could be diabetic and she could give him an insulin overdose in his coffee; it'd be impossible to trace."[150]

Funny and sad at the same time, isn't it?

When Ruth Graham, wife of world evangelist Billy Graham, was asked if she had ever thought of divorcing her husband during their marriage, she said: "Divorce? No. Murder. Yes."[151]

My sister Maria was shocked and horrified when I admitted once that I sometimes think of Ray's funeral when I'm really mad at him. She said that was weird and disturbing. Of course, I've always repented after the thoughts and asked God's forgiveness. I don't entertain these thoughts (long!). I have a few married friends who've confessed that they've thought similar thoughts about their husbands.

In the movie *Heartburn*, Rachel (played by Meryl Streep, my favorite actress) discovers that her husband Mark (actor Jack Nicholson) has been having an affair with Thelma Rice, "someone who is very tall," as she describes her to her father's cleaning woman/babysitter.

One day Rachel is crying, talking on the phone with her best friend Julie (Stockard Channing), who sympathizes because she understands Rachel's pain. Julie says that when she found out about her husband Arthur's affair, she fantasized about his funeral, what she'd wear at the funeral, and flirting with other men at the funeral.

Ray has admitted that when he's extremely angry at me, he has (wishfully) thought about me dying, too.

What's the matter with us? I think it's a way to try to cope. We just want the pain to stop, right? I have no doubt at all that in times of "intense domestic fellowship"—the humorous phrase coined by our friends Don and Gala Palmgren for marital strife—Ray has daydreamed many times of being consoled by family and friends at my funeral, and of giving the eulogy so he could have the last, final word with me.

## For Better or for Worse

Seriously, marriage is one of the biggest testing grounds for Christian believers. Many times we are attracted to our opposites. Initially during the dating or courtship period, we like this. You're intrigued by the differences and appreciate them. They add the salt and the spice to the relationship, and you learn from each other.

After marriage, those differences become the reason for escalated arguments resembling Oliver's (Michael Douglas) and Barbara's (Kathleen Turner) raging, ultimately fatal fighting in *The War of the Roses* movie.[152]

I believe the reason for the fighting and the hurts boils down to three things:

- Communication problems/misunderstandings
- Shattered expectations
- Selfishness

## Communication Problems/Misunderstandings

Studies show that there are differences in the way males and females communicate.[153] Here are examples of some of those differences, which can result in "intense domestic fellowship" between a husband and a wife:

- He believes communication should have a clear purpose; she communicates to discover how she's feeling and what she wants to say, and to build intimacy;

- He values productivity and efficiency and wonders why she has to talk so freaking much, because he's already eliminated the muck in his head before speaking.

She uses communication to explore and organize her thoughts…and she has *lots* of thoughts and ideas!

- He's conditioned to listen actively and assumes when she initiates conversation, she wants his wise, amazing advice. She just wants to talk with someone to heal from her hurts, encourage her, and equip her to handle the world and its trials. It just makes her feel better to talk!

- He wants to tackle problems head-on, like a fireman, putting the fire out by giving solutions. She isn't asking him to solve her problems, but just to be a sounding board. Why is she coming to him if she doesn't want his help? And why is she giving him all these details? Just get to the point already!

- He also may take her mood personally, as if she's mad or upset with him, and defends himself if she starts getting all emotional. Oh no, not the tears again! He can't stand it when she cries; it makes him feel so helpless! But when he expresses support or shows concern for her feelings, she feels loved and he's fulfilling her primary love need. Sometimes all she needs is a hug or him to say, "I love you" or "I'm here for you."

- He de-stresses by withdrawing into his man cave, becoming quiet and withdrawn. He forgets problems by focusing on other things like watching TV, playing videos, or hanging out with buddies, drinking beer. She interprets his silence and withdrawal as she's failing him or she's losing him. But giving him space shows him she trusts him. Meanwhile she should do something to nurture herself, so she doesn't resent him for his cave time.

- He feels like she's acting like his mother and he's being

told what to do. He becomes hurt when his competency is questioned, and throws up a wall of resistance. (Ray calls it me being "the expert on everything.") When she's upset about something and he tells her that she's making a mountain out of a molehill, she feels he's minimizing her feelings and uncaring—"What a jerk!"[154] Can you see why we have problems communicating.

**Just the Facts, Ma'am**

Men generally don't like details; women do. Learning about and understanding these differences will help couples get unstuck from communication roadblocks.

Communication difficulties, left unresolved and/or ignored, can grow into intense strife, unforgiveness, bitterness, resentment, hatred, contempt, disrespect, and finally the worst of all—apathy. If problems aren't dealt with effectively and quickly, one day you'll be looking across the kitchen table at a distant stranger. I can tell you that isn't a fun or a good place to be, because it's where Ray and I are at now.

Personally, I believe that daily forgiveness is one of the biggest problems married couples face. As my therapist sister Maria says, what happens is that couples "stockpile" offenses, when each day they should start over, wipe off everything on the board of their hearts and have a clean slate. God's mercies are new each morning;[155] ours should be, too, if we're His kids.

Times of needed forgiveness are when the marriage covenant vows are tried most. The promise a husband and a wife make to each other at the altar "until death do us part" is tested severely. You just want to give up and quit! You never thought it'd be this hard.

Statistically, over 50 percent of married couples divorce, even among Christian marriages. In addition, 60 to 63 percent of second marriages and 70 to 73 percent of third marriages end in divorce.

Marriage's promises may not last. The good news is that even if your marriage crumbles and you divorce, your life isn't over.[156]

In the movie *Under the Tuscan Sun*,[157] Frances' divorce attorney tells her that her husband is seeking alimony from her and his girlfriend wants their house as she really likes the place—because, adding insult to injury, she's pregnant and there's good schools near their home for their child to attend.

The attorney tells Frances, "You're gonna' get over this. You will, Frances. Someday, you're going to be happy again."

She just nods, saying "Right," with tears falling down her face.

The good news is that even if your marriage doesn't last, God's love and promises stand forever.

## Shattered Expectations

My husband Ray was given a beautiful picture of marriage as he was growing up. The example I was given was one of mixture. My parents stayed married until my mother's death when I was eighteen years old. They were committed to each other, but looking back, I wouldn't describe their marriage as very happy. I never saw real open displays of love, affection, and closeness between them.

I knew somehow that my mother loved my father (I guess because she was more physically affectionate with him than he was with her), but I didn't think he loved her as much as she loved him.

They also argued at times. My mom would slam the back door and tear off in the car to go secretly smoke a cigarette at my paternal grandmother's house.

She'd come back home, calmed down.

They didn't argue in front of us four kids, but occasionally we'd hear them arguing late at night—mostly over money. But they stayed together.

When mama died, I was shocked to see my father crying quietly over her in the casket and realized he really did love her.

Ray's parents' marriage was very unhappy. When he was twelve years old, his parents went through a painful divorce. He spent a lot of summers at his maternal grandparents Hutchins' home, who were a great role model for marriage and Christianity. They were faithfully married for over forty years until his Grandmother Hutchins died of cancer. Several years later, his grandfather died. Ray wanted a solid, great, happy marriage like theirs.

Some of Ray's and his mother Judy's fondest memories of grandmother Hutchins were that she wore a dress, high heels and pearls even when vacuuming, cooking, and cleaning at home.

"She always looked like a lady," Judy said.

Grandmother Hutchins would cook a warm breakfast and make coffee for Ray's grandfather Hutchins each morning. She'd also cook a delicious supper for him after his long, hard day at work. This is the memory that stands out the most about her to Ray. This is the picture on which he bases his view of "a good wife." (So I've miserably failed!)

Ray's grandfather often had long talks with "his boy" and would tell Ray that no matter how much she could frustrate him at times, he sure loved that woman. Marriage bliss.

Then enter reality! Ray met me when he was in his late twenties. I was a single mother, and our typical "meals" were hot dogs, peanut butter and jelly sandwiches, pizza, and tuna melt sandwiches. I mixed mustard with the tuna, which grossed out and horrified Ray. If he's forced to eat tuna because there's no other food in the house (Ray is a meat and potatoes man), he only eats it with mayonnaise, chopped up onion, and relish. Heather and I also loved to eat at McDonald's, which Ray finds disgusting and can't stand to eat. (We rarely go to McDonald's now. But I'm very into Mexican food!)

Back then, I barely knew how to cook, and even worse, I hated doing it and had no desire to learn.

Ray's ideal for a wife was a Grandmother Hutchins-type southern cook, a June Cleaver perfect housekeeper/mom for the kids, and a hot, Jennifer Aniston, arm-candy wife, all rolled into one. It was an expectation I couldn't possibly fulfill. No woman could.

## Set Your Cornflakes on Fire

Marriage expert/author Gary Smalley has told the funny story in his *Love Is A Decision* marriage seminars about his wife Norma's angry reply once that if he wanted a hot breakfast, to set his cornflakes on fire. It always makes me laugh. I relate.

For over twenty years, Ray and I have gone round and round about the cooking issue. I know that a good, godly wife would do this for her dedicated, hard-working husband. It's just that I HATE to cook! To me, standing over a hot stove for hours (or even half an hour!) is akin to Chinese water torture.

That is why I love eating out so much. I don't have to cook and get hot. It's fast. It's easy. And if you choose the right place, it tastes great. What a deal!

My favorite restaurants in town are the Mexican restaurant El Charro (chips and salsa, chicken fajitas with rice and beans, and a big Coke, please!) or the mom-and-pop type restaurant Flaming Lantern, where I usually order a Reuben sandwich and a half order of fries.

Just so you don't think that we eat out every day, we don't. We only eat out a few times every two weeks when Ray gets his paycheck. I eat lots of salads at home. We also eat a lot of tacos, chicken dishes, and a simple casserole Ray makes called cheesy mac (extra cheesy macaroni and cheese, cooked lean ground beef, and a can of mild rotel tomatoes, all mixed together, salted, peppered, and spiced— Leah loves it). Occasionally I try new recipes, especially in the Crock-Pot, which I think is one of the greatest inventions ever made for women!

Through the years, I've learned to cook more dishes. Yes, I've improved my cooking skills by much trial and error, but I'm still not great at it. A few dishes Ray has raved about and requested, like my homemade potato and leek soup and homemade chili. I make a delicious, extra-cheesy (with green olives) meat loaf. Once I made homemade ravioli that was simply to die for...and Ray almost did. I was actually cooking something that had more than three ingredients!

Yes, I confess: I still hate cooking to this day. There are a thousand other things I'd rather do in life! No, I'll never be a gourmet chef. No, I'll never be a Grandmother Hutchins.

I am still *so not* a morning person, who "gets up while it is still night; she provides food for her family." Are you kidding me? This is Ray's greatest woe about me. He has finally stopped hoping I'll do it. The poor man.

I cook *sometimes* (just not breakfast at the crack of dawn!). At other times, Ray cooks. He's actually a much better cook than I am. He's one of those people who can throw a few things together with spices and it turns out great. (Just not his goulash!)

He's *incredible* on the grill. One of the reasons I married him was because of his Cajun chicken that he cooks on the grill. He's famous for it among family and friends. It is so delicious! When he grills steaks, they are perfect—thick, medium rare, juicy, tender.

He also makes a sweet holiday ham each Thanksgiving and Christmas, which our kids specifically request. They love dad's ham!

Cleaning, though—he's not so good at that.

I'm good at cleaning, but not so much at cooking. I need to be more diligent with cooking. Sometimes, especially if I'm busy working long hours on a speaking presentation or writing on my laptop, *nobody* cooks, and Ray or Leah will knock on my office door and ask forlornly: "Do you have any plans for dinner tonight or do we have to fend for ourselves?"

This always makes me feel so bad. What kind of woman is too busy for and doesn't like to cook for her own family? These are usually "pizza nights"!

## Breakfast at Tiffany's

Ray and I have never really resolved the breakfast issue. I have a hard enough time even waking up in the morning and speaking civilly to people, much less cooking at sunrise. I am not a morning person, and cheerful morning people get on my last nerve. Ray knows not to say to me, "Good morning!" because I might bite his head off. Just being real here!

Several years ago, Ray and I traveled to Israel, my dream come true. We both delighted in the delicious food, served at a beautifully set table, for every meal wherever we went. Breakfast was always a feast. We missed that when we came back home.

At times throughout our marriage, I've tried to recapture the romantic experience and good memories of that trip. I've set the alarm and cooked Ray's breakfast: fried or scrambled eggs, bacon, warm bread with a variety of cheeses, with a pot of good, strong, hot coffee. I set Ray's Grandmother Forte's cream pitcher and sugar dish on the table for an added special touch. I find whatever fresh fruit is in season: bananas, peaches, mangoes, or strawberries, and slice them, to add a touch of color.

But most of the time, I don't cook breakfast for him. A better wife would. I repent in dust and ashes.

Ray's expectation was that when he married me, I would cook like his Grandmother Hutchins cooked breakfast and other meals for his Granddad Hutchins. Ray has had shattered expectations being married to me. All the man wants to do is eat.

My expectations have been shattered like glass, too. Most married couples' are.

The cooking has been only one issue of our marriage. There have been other much more serious issues, such as:

- The hospital intern who had sex with me the first year of our marriage.

- Ray's pornography addiction to hardcore Internet porn the second year of marriage.

- Ray's period of unemployment the first year of our marriage and several years ago for an entire year, resulting in severe financial problems, stress, and strife.

- As a result of his job loss several years ago, our home foreclosed, my SUV was repossessed, and we had to file complete bankruptcy.

- Intense conflicts between me and his daughter, Eden, from his previous marriage.

- Ray being asked to step down (fired!) from church leadership due to our intense marital and financial problems, which was humiliating for both of us.

- And much, much more…years filled with intense and constant arguing, unforgiveness, bitterness, disillusionment, and many sorrowful tears. It's been a long, hard road and it feels as if we have no destination in sight…just more years of the same old, same old, that mountain we keep going around. A road neither of us wants to travel. Did Ray and I make a wrong turn when we married? Did we make a big mistake?

I've often thought, *This was not the life I signed up for, God!* Do you relate?

## Promises In The Dark

Speaker/author Donna Partow describes a recurring nightmare she has where she's sitting down to take a final exam in biochemistry or nuclear physics, when she thought she signed up for basket weaving. What she assumed to be a no-brainer was the ultimate test. Her classmates are zipping along, while she stares blankly at the page and waves of fear and insecurity sweep over her as the reality hits her that she's completely unprepared.

> Sometimes life can feel like that. We suddenly find ourselves faced with a challenging exam—like cancer, a prodigal child, or the loss of a loved one. We want to cry out, "Hey, God, this isn't the life I signed up for! I specifically remember signing up for great parents, a great marriage, and great kids who rise up and call me blessed. I signed up for lifelong friendships, thin thighs, and vibrant health. Instead I find myself in the middle of a life I DIDN'T sign up for. My husband says he doesn't love me anymore. My daughter just pierced her tongue. The bills are stacked a mile high, and my company just announced another round of layoffs. To top it all off, I'm forty pounds overweight and my doctor says I'm a heart attack waiting to happen....The obvious truth is: No one asks for the challenges of life. But in the real world, tough times are inevitable. We all want to live happily ever after.[158]

We often look to marriage as the ultimate promise being fulfilled. You know, "*Happily ever after.*" It's like Cinderella dancing with the Prince at the ball.

Yeah, right! Instead, we often experience the greatest depths of hurt in our life. More *promises in the dark*—the darkness of disappointment.

Yet marriage is God's elite training ground for forming us into the image of Jesus Christ and maturing us in faith. He's the Potter and we are the clay. Marriage is the perfect school of the Holy Spirit for learning forgiveness and agape love:

> God has provided a remarkable solution: a love directed and fueled, not by the emotions, but by the will. Out of His own mighty nature, God supplies the resources for this love, and they are available to any life connected with His by faith in Jesus Christ…This is the agape love of the New Testament – unconditional, unchanging, inexhaustible, generous beyond measure, and most wonderfully kind.[159]

## God Always Keeps His Promises

We have to remember our spouses are human, not God. Your husband is going to screw up, sometimes a lot. You will, too! We have to surrender our high—even impossible—expectations of our spouse to God. Lay them down at the foot of the cross. He or she is not perfect and never will be. Practice understanding, self-control and patience. Walk in love and forgiveness. The only way you can do this is by God's grace.

Yes, your husband made vows at the altar to always love, honor and cherish you. Some days he won't. At times he'll be rude, selfish, stingy, and/or mean. Sin, that original battle in a perfect garden, often causes him to act this way. He needs to repent!

At other times, his behavior is because he's exhausted from work, he doesn't feel well, he's preoccupied with worries, and/or his back and shoulders hurt. Ask God for discernment and insight into your husband's behavior.

Try to empathize and be understanding when he's grumpy. Sometimes when Ray is real irritable and impatient with me, I realize it's not personal: he just got off a twenty-four-hour shift at the hospital and didn't get any sleep during his down time there. What he needs is to go to bed and rest.

Go the extra mile. Give him a back oil massage. Cook his favorite meal or dessert like a key lime pie. Buy him a new Kindle Fire or a pair of the finest quality cowboy boots.

You might feel like yelling or hitting him when he's acting like the world's biggest jerk, but instead ask God for grace to love and respect him. To show him Christ's light.

Your husband or your wife *will* disappoint you at times. But God never will disappoint you. He is faithful and true.[160] His promises are yes and amen.[161] They stand forever.[162]

God's everlasting arms of love are under you.[163] The Lord your Maker is your husband.[164] God will never forsake or abandon you.

> Be strong. Take courage. Don't be intimidated. Don't give them a second thought because God, your God, is striding ahead of you. He's right there with you. He won't let you down; he won't leave you.[165]

Right now I'm going through a very difficult time in our marriage. Ray and I have been married for over twenty-one years, and it has been hell. We've been on the edge of divorce for years, but are trying to hang on to honor our vows to God and each other, and to be an example to our children, grandchildren, and others about commitment in marriage. We're in pastoral counseling now with our small group leaders Dave and Ruth Christian to restore our marriage. We are praying weekly with Dave, who is counseling us, and we're praying for each other daily.

Dave felt that God gave him a "prescription" for our marriage's restoration and healing, if we are willing—the scripture about the man who had been waiting thirty-eight years by the pool to be healed.

When the angel stirred the waters, people were miraculously healed.

> When Jesus saw him lying there, and knew that he already had been in that condition a long time, He said to him, "Do you want to be made well?" The sick man answered Him, "Sir, I have no man to put me into the pool when the water is stirred up; but while I am coming, another steps down before me." Jesus said to him, "Rise, take up your bed and walk." And immediately the man was made well, too up his bed, and walked.[166]

Ray and I have to be willing to be healed, to change and repent. To be honest, I don't know if our marriage is going to last or not. I pray it does, for the sake of our vow to God, the missions/ministry call that is on our life together, and for our children and our grandchildren. Our friends (at least a few of them, who are devout Christians) want to see our marriage succeed, too. As Dave says, much is at stake here—even people's souls. I also don't want to give Satan the satisfaction of having destroyed our marriage! He has stolen enough! I also know my husband is God's gift to me.

For Dave's prescription, we are reading Stormie O'Martian's books *The Power of a Praying Husband* and *The Power of a Praying Wife*, and praying the prayers from each chapter over each other.

We're also reading Gary Chapman's book *The Five Love Languages* to discover our own and each other's love language, and to express love in that love language daily.

A successful, happy marriage is a little more complicated than giving a back rub or a buying some chocolate, though. Why is marriage so challenging? Why couldn't God have made this a lot easier and simpler?

It's hard to keep your promise to someone who is constantly hurting you.

I think Ray is going to get an amazing reward in heaven from God for putting up with me so long. At the same time, this marriage has been extremely emotionally painful for me. Ray has hurt me more than any other man in my life.

Yet I hold on in faith and hope...

> Allie: Do you think that our love can create miracles?
> Noah: Yes, I do. That's what brings you back to me each time.
> Allie: Do you think our love can take us away together?
> Noah: I think our love can do anything we want it to.
> —*The Notebook* movie

> I am here to love you, to hold you in my arms, to protect you.
> —*Message in a Bottle* movie

Recently our daughter Leah and I went to Chick-Fil-A for lunch. While there, I noticed a beautiful, young wife and mom with her husband and two kids at a table nearby. She would occasionally glance over at me. When they were ready to go, her husband led their children outside to their car.

As Leah and I stood up to leave, she went out the door at the same time as us and I commented on how beautiful her children were. She said they actually had five children and were such blessings. I agreed. This conversation about her kids opened the door for her to speak prophetically into my life, although she didn't even know me.

She told me she felt that God wanted me to know that He is my Husband[167] and He loves me deeply. She shared other words that were spot on which greatly blessed me. This accurate prophetic word was timely and encouraging, and tears filled my eyes.

God sees everything we are going through in our lives: our pain, our heartaches, and our sorrows. He collects our tears in His bottle; He records each one in His book.[168]

Marriage is hard. Let's face it—it can be hell. The hardest thing you might ever do. You will want to give up, to quit, probably many times. Many people do. It's a sad testimony that as many Christians as unbelievers are divorcing or are divorced. Just today, I heard on Facebook that a friend of mine is going through a divorce; she and her husband are Christians. I don't know the details yet, but I do know, Satan now has another victory.

Don't let that be you. The way I look at it, I'm not going to give the devil the evil satisfaction of destroying my marriage. He's stolen enough from my life as it is. It's time to take back the land. With God nothing is impossible. He can turn the broken into beautiful for His glory.

Sometimes your husband or your wife will not keep the promises of his/her marriage vows. But God *always* keeps His promises to you. He is faithful, even when we are not.

## Promises In The Dark

## Chapter 7

# just jesus
# the glass slipper

*"If there's anyone who can appear before Aslan without their knees knocking, they're either braver than most, or else just silly."*
*~ C.S. Lewis, The Lion, The Witch, and The Wardrobe ~*

*The Lion, The Witch, and the Wardrobe* is one of our family's favorite movies. We read C. S. Lewis' books first when I was homeschooling Leah, and then the new Andrew Adamson's Chronicles movies came out. The lion Aslan, who represents Jesus the Lion of Judah, was a beloved character to us and our kids. As Mr. Beaver said, He is not safe, but He is good. Yes, God is always good! And He's everything to me.

I don't know how atheists or agnostics do it, living without God. I couldn't go on one second apart from Him. The Bible says in Acts 17:28, "For in Him we live and move and have our being."

Oh, I tried for years to live without Him. The results were disastrous with lots of painful regrets. When you go your own way, you wind up moving around aimlessly in circles, like the Israelites going around the wilderness forty years, and one day you muse,

> *I just look around and say, "I'm a mess. I don't know why I do things."*
> *~ Mike Tyson ~*

Yep, my life was a big, fat mess! I'm really good at making messes. Right now my desk is a mess and I need to organize it. But I don't respond well to clutter. Chaos around me makes me feel chaotic inside. Sin is spiritual chaos that bleeds into all areas of our lives.

Only God can clean up your and my messes and make them into beautiful messages. Only God can take the chaos of my life and yours, turn it around 180, and use it to display His glory. From chaos to *charis* (*charis* is the Greek word for blessing, favor, gift, grace, thankfulness).

It's extraordinary to me that God can use my messes as a blessing to others! In fact, God forms our testimony into a powerful weapon against the enemy Satan:

> They had power over him and won because of the blood of the Lamb and by telling what He had done for them. They did not love their lives but were willing to die.[169]

It's not about what we have done wrong in our lives, but about what Jesus has done for us on the cross over 2,000 years ago. His life in exchange for ours. Our sin in exchange for God's forgiveness and Jesus' perfection.

A Divine, extraordinary, miraculous exchange by God's sheer grace. It's just unfathomable; how can we be anything but grateful to Him for what He's done? His promises seem too good to be true, but they are true—forever! God has given us promises in His word that never fail. The Bible has many beautiful precious promises for you and me, but there are seven that are extremely encouraging:

- **Eternal life**. One of the things that God has promised me which really comforts me is that I won't be burning in the lake of fire in hell forever because of my sins! It's mind-blowing, really, that God is just that good to me. I know I don't deserve His goodness, and that I should've died and gone to hell a long time ago. And it's so much more than that: God has also promised me abundant life through Christ.

"My sheep recognize My voice. I know them, and they follow Me. I give them real and eternal life. They are protected from the Destroyer for good." (John 10:27-28, The Message)[170] Are you experiencing the good, abundant life through Christ?

- **Forgiveness of sins and the gift of the Holy Spirit**. I am so not perfect. I'm good at falling and failing, without even trying very hard.

  I relate to what national speaker/author Beth Moore (who has my maiden name, ironically), wrote in her book, *Believing God*: "…if I die suddenly, my gravestone might appropriately offer this insight into my departure: "God got tired." I require lots of work."

  I think I wear God out, too. He's so patient! God wants to change my life and yours for the better—and our children's. I'm so thankful for God's forgiveness.

  Peter said, "Change your life. Turn to God and be baptized, each of you, in the name of Jesus Christ, so your sins are forgiven. Receive the gift of the Holy Spirit. The promise is targeted to you and your children, but also to all who are far away – whomever, in fact, our Master God invites." (Acts 2:38, The Message)

- **Victory over death**. For many years I was terrified of dying and going to hell for my abortions, adultery, and other sins, even though I was saved. Satan was tormenting me with fear through the weapon of condemnation. If Jesus is our Lord and Savior, we don't need to be afraid of dying or of death, because we are sealed by His Holy Spirit and we'll spend eternity with God in heaven. We don't have to fear His judgment, because all our sins were judged at and paid for at the Cross by Jesus.

O death, where is your victory? O death, where is your sting? (Hosea 13:14)

For sin is the sting that results in death, and the law gives sin its power. But thank God! He gives us victory over sin and death through our Lord Jesus Christ. (1 Corinthians 15:56-57, NLT)

- **God's grace is enough for you**. Ever had one of those days where everything was going wrong? Ever had one of those years, or lives?! God didn't say it would be easy. Jesus' life wasn't easy. He was ridiculed, mocked, insulted, falsely accused, betrayed by a friend, abandoned by His best friends just when He needed them the most, and then tortured and crucified. How's that for victorious Christian living?

  Yet it was God's will! The secret to Jesus overcoming the trials in this life and even death on the cross was His absolute dependence on and surrender to God, sustained by grace.

  Whenever you feel overwhelmed and like you just can't go on for another second, remember that God has a fresh supply of grace for you. Come to Him. Just talk to Him about your problems. He will help you, refresh you, and refill you with His living waters.

Each time He said, "My grace is all you need. My power works best in weakness." So now I am glad to boast about my weaknesses, so that the power of Christ can work through me. (2 Corinthians 12:9, NLT)

- **Help to overcome temptation**. I don't know about you, but I'm easily tempted: things like chocolate, Mexican food, Coke, pretty new clothes and shoes, and other not-so-pleasant things like impatience, anger, fear, and discouragement.

  Every day I need God's power to overcome areas of temptation. He wants to give you and me that help in our weak area, which is different for each of us. I may struggle with frequently feeling discouraged; someone else may struggle with lust. But we all need Jesus to be victorious! Through Christ you are an overcomer!

  Listen to Mandisa's song Overcomer at this link: http://www.youtube.com/watch?v=b8VoUYtx0kw

  No test or temptation that comes your way is beyond the course of what others have had to face. All you need to remember is that God will never let you down; He'll never let you be pushed past your limit; He'll always be there to help you come through it. (1 Corinthians 10:13, The Message)

- **Provision for everything we need**. The key word here is *need*, not want. God hasn't promised you a big screen TV, a new Porsche luxury car, or even a wonderful, trouble-free marriage.

God's promise to provide all we need doesn't mean we won't struggle sometimes. Remember that without the struggle, the caterpillar would never strengthen her wings to become a butterfly and be free to fly. Without problems in our lives, we'd never learn to look to, depend on and trust in God.

Ray and I have intensely struggled financially at times throughout our marriage, but God has never let us or our children starve. At times the bank account has been low and we've craved Mexican food, Chick-Fil-A, or a medium rare steak with a loaded baked potato instead of ramen noodles, tuna casserole or tacos, but God hasn't ever let us starve. In fact, many times He has given us *abundance*, blessing us in ways we certainly didn't deserve.

And my God will give you everything you need because of His great riches in Christ Jesus. (Philippians 4:19, NLV)

I love the Amplified Bible's version of this verse which says, "And my God will liberally supply (*fill to the full*) your every need according to His riches in glory in Christ Jesus."

I believe that God wants to not only provide for our needs, but to also bless and prosper us. To learn more about this, go to the following link for my ebook, *That You Would Prosper as Your Soul Prospers*: http://www.bethjones.net/prosper-ebook/

- **He'll work everything for our good and His glory.** This is one of the things that people say when you're going through hard times which is so irritating, isn't it? But it's true and I've seen its evidence first-hand in my life.

  I was sexually and physically abused as a child in

horrendous ways, but God has done amazing healing in my life and used my childhood abuse to minister to women in nations all over the world, who've been through similar, painful things. I share some of my story in my book, *The Hands Of A Woman: Everyday Women In Everyday Battles*. To learn more, go to: http://womensbattles.com/.

My life seems to have been like *A Series of Unfortunate Events*,[171] yet God has chosen to use many of these places of my deepest pain to set other women free.

And we know that in all things God works for the good of those who love Him, who have been called according to His purpose. (Romans 8:28, NIV)

One day what you're going through will be worth it all. Listen to Rita Springer's song, *Worth It All* here: http://www.youtube.com/watch?v=BQVmR0jV52A&list=PL485371396C3E250B

There are many wonderful promises in the Bible for you and me. According to one person's count, there are 3,573 promises. The word *promise* occurs thirteen times in the King James version Bible.[172]

I think one of the most beautiful stories in the Bible is the promise God made to Abraham and Sarah for a male son. Abram (his name later changed to "Abraham") had obeyed God and God had given everything he needed.

In Genesis 15: 4-5, God appeared to Abraham in a vision and told him not to be afraid because He would protect him, and that He was Abraham's reward.

Abram agreed that God had given him some great stuff (my paraphrase), but what good did all that do when he didn't have any kids—no one to leave it to but his servant Eliezer? Abram and Sarai were too old to have any children. Abram's desire was to have his own son. If God's promise were to come true, he had to have a son. God told Abram to look up into the sky at the stars and that's how many descendants he'd have.

Did you know that no one knows how many stars there are? Astrophysicists at NASA estimate there to be around $10^{21}$ stars in the universe. That's 1,000,000,000,000,000,000,000![173]

That's a lot of kids. Talk about a big family!

Abram and Sarai had to wait twenty-five years before the "fullness of time" in which God promised them a son. Have you ever been waiting on a promise that seemed to take forever? I know I have. In fact, the waiting was so hard that Sarai decided to take matters into her own hands, and told Abram to have sex with her maid Hagar to get them a son. (This was a practice among barren couples in that culture, as being childless was shameful. It was also the only way to pass down a man's inheritance and legacy of faith.)

What was wrong with that woman? Ray would sleep with another woman over my dead body! We find out later how many problems the unbelief in their hearts and this foolish decision caused them.

But Abram didn't seem to mind too much or object to Sarai's lunatic idea, so he slept with Hagar the maid and conceived his son Ishmael through her. Yet Ishmael was not the promised heir.

In Genesis 18, God again promises Abram a son and that he will be the father of a new nation. God changes Abram's name to "Abraham" and Sarai's to "Sarah."

Abram fell facedown, and God said to him, "As for Me, this is My covenant with you: you will be the father of many nations; I will make you very fruitful; I will make nations of you, and kings will come from you. I will establish My covenant as an everlasting covenant between me and you and your descendants after you for the generations to come, to be your God and the God of your descendants after you."

God means what He says and says what He means. God's promises are "yes" and "amen."[174]

God isn't like humans; He never lies.[175] He will fulfill His promises to you!

In Genesis 18, the Lord appeared to Abraham and three heavenly visitors dropped by to see him before going to destroy Sodom and Gomorrah with fire. Abraham hurriedly had a servant prepare them something to eat and drink and as they were eating, one of them asked where Sarah was. He told him she was in the tent. The visitor then told Abraham by this time next year, Sarah would have a son.

In the tent, Sarah started cracking up laughing because by this time, she and Abraham were very old and were past the time to have children.

"How could a worn-out woman like me enjoy such pleasure, especially when my master—my husband—is also so old?" Sarah asked, laughing.[176]

> Not too smart to laugh at God. He always gets the last laugh anyway.[177]
>
> What God has prepared for you is bigger and better than you can even think. Cinderella's glass slippers enabled her to experience a destiny she had never even thought possible:
>
> God can do anything, you know—far more than you could ever imagine or guess or request in your wildest dreams! He does it not by pushing us around but by working within us, His Spirit deeply and gently within us.[178]
>
> The next year, Abraham and Sarah did have the son whom God promised—Isaac, whose name means "laughter." Abraham became the father of a great nation, the Jews of Israel, as many as the stars, just as God promised him.
>
> Can you imagine the joy that Abraham and Sarah felt holding that precious, beautiful baby boy? He was their miracle child! They'd waited so long to have children—twenty-five years! But God is never late on His promises; He's always right on time!

The world offers many promises, but many times comes up empty. I've been lured by those promises for years. As a result, I've experienced deep disappointment, hurt, heartbreak, and regret.

Yet with God I've never been disappointed. I can always count on Him. So can you. God's promises are faithful and forever true.

God makes beautiful things out of brokenness.

Thank you, God, You can do that even with me.

# Call to Action Steps...
# For You To Believe In and Trust God's Promises

**Spend consistent, daily quiet time with God.** Pray, worship and praise Him. Read, study and meditate on the Bible. Listen for His still, quiet voice to speak to your heart. Elijah heard God not in the wind, the earthquake, or the fire but in the still, small voice. (1 Kings 19: 9-15)

God wants to have an intimate relationship with you. The way you get to know and trust someone is by spending time with him or her. Set aside a regular time every day (it doesn't have to be early morning and it can be just fifteen to thirty minutes) and a room in your home (a prayer room, your bedroom, or even a corner of the family room) for a quiet time place to spend with God. As you grow and mature in your understanding of God, you'll come to trust His promises for your life. He is faithful.

**Obey God.** God blesses us when we have child-like faith, trust, and obey Him. Abraham was called the "friend of God" and received His promises because he simply believed God and did what He said.

The more time you spend with God and in His word, and come to understand how much He loves you, the more you'll desire to obey Him. You'll become humbled at how He longs to shower you with His goodness (despite yourself, even after you've messed up!), and want to please Him and do what is right.

As you continue walking in obedience to Him, you'll experience showers of His blessings.

> I will make them and the places surrounding my hill a blessing. I will send down showers in season; there will be showers of blessing. (Ezekiel 34:26, NIV)

**Remember what He's done.** The patriarchs made altars of memorial stones to reflect on and remember what God had done in their lives. (Genesis 28: 12-22, Genesis 31: 43-55, Joshua 4).

You can write in your journal how God has answered prayers in your life.

Years ago Ray gave me a beautiful wooden prayer box that had little white cards inside it, to write down my prayer requests. Later I could write down the date when the prayer was answered and how God answered it. It serves as a beautiful, precious memorial to me how God is working miraculously each day in our family's lives. You could make your own prayer box with index cards or pretty paper, or use another creative process such as drawing and painting as a memorial. Writing a book is a memorial to God, also.

Best of all, you can verbally share stories with your children and grandchildren to leave a legacy of faith in Jesus Christ. Your children, your grandchildren and the generations to come if Jesus tarries are your inheritance.

> Behold, I and the children whom the Lord has given me are for signs and for wonders in Israel from the Lord of hosts, which dwells in mount Zion. (Isaiah 8:18, AKJV)

I was so blessed this weekend to see our granddaughter Violet (eight years old) being baptized with other members of their church. As I watched my precious daughter Heather go into the pool with Violet, her hands on her shoulders, tears filled my eyes and deep joy filled my heart. Not only does Heather believe in and serve Jesus Christ, but now her children do as well. I have a righteous legacy of faith in Jesus through my children and grandchildren!

> Like arrows in the hands of a warrior, are children born in one's youth. (Psalm 127:4, NIV)

God's promises are for real and forever! Amen!

PROMISES IN THE DARK

# ENDNOTES

[1] *When A Woman Finds Her Voice: Overcoming Life's Hurts and Using Your Story to Make a Difference*, Jo Ann Fore, Leafwood Publishers, October 8, 2013.

[2] Antimony forms **a highly useful alloy with lead, increasing its hardness and mechanical strength**. Antimony compounds are prominent additives for chlorine- and bromine-containing **fire retardants** found in many commercial and domestic products. Source: http://en.wikipedia.org/wiki/Antimony. God wants his women strong!

[3] Isaiah 54:11, ESV.

[4] Ephesians 4:29, King James 2000 Bible.

[5] Proverbs 15:23, King James 2000 Bible.

[6] *Message In A Bottle*, http://www.imdb.com/title/tt0139462/

[7] 2 Corinthians 4:7, NLT.

[8] *A Tale of Three Kings: A Study in Brokenness*, Gene Edwards, Tyndale House Publishers, May 21, 1992.

[9] *Gone With The Wind*, Margaret Mitchell, MacMillan, 1936.

[10] *Side Effects of Insomnia*, http://signsofinsomnia.org/side-effects-of-insomnia/.

[11] What is cutting, http://www.wisegeek.com/what-is-cutting.htm.

[12] Revelations 19:12.

[13] Numbers 23:19.

[14] Hebrews 13:5.

[15] Isaiah 49:16.

[16] John 8: 1-11, The Message.

[17] Jeremiah 29:11.

[18] 1 Corinthians 2:9.

[19] *My Only Sunshine,* http://en.wikipedia.org/wiki/You_Are_My_Sunshine.

[20] *When A Woman Finds Her Voice: Overcoming Life's Hurts & Using Your Story To Make A Difference,* Jo Ann Fore, Leafwood Publishers, Abilene, TS, 2013, p. 36.

[21] Genesis 50:10, NIV.

[22] Isaiah 61:3.

[23] Beth Jones, International Speaker, http://www.bethjones.net/speaking/speaking-topics/.

[24] Isaiah 61:10, MSG.

[25] *Happily Ever After,* Toben & Joanne Heim, Kregel Publications, Grand Rapids, MI, 2006, p. 70.

[26] *Looking Forward*, "The Simple Wife," February 25, 2014, Joanne Heim, http://thesimplewife.typepad.com/the_simple_wife/2014/02/-looking-forward-joanne.html.

[27] Ibid, Joanne Heim.

[28] Song of Solomon 2:15.

[29] *Eat, Pray, Love*, Elizabeth Gilbert, http://www.goodreads.com/author/quotes/11679.Elizabeth_Gilbert.

[30] Ibid.

[31] Romans 7:14-24, NLT.

[32] *I Still Haven't Found What I'm Looking For*, U2, The Joshua Tree album, http://en.wikipedia.org/wiki/I_Still_Haven%27t_Found_What_I%27m_Looking_For.

[33] Isaiah 43:2, NLT.

[34] *What Is Cutting*, WiseGeek, http://www.wisegeek.com/what-is-cutting.htm.

[35] James 5:16, NLT.

[36] Psalm 68:6, NLT.

[37] *Amazing Grace*, John Newton, Published 1779.

[38] *Attention Hyperactivity Deficit Disorder*, PubMed Health, http://www.ncbi.nlm.nih.gov/pubmedhealth/PMH0002518/.

[39] "Remarriage, Children of Divorce," *Journal of the American Board of Family Members*, http://www.medscape.com/viewarticle/405852_7.

[40] Hebrews 12:6.

[41] *Attention Hyperactivity Deficit Disorder*, PubMed Health, http://www.ncbi.nlm.nih.gov/pubmedhealth/PMH0002518/.

[42] *18 Shocking Children and Divorce Statistics*, Larry Bilotta, http://www.marriage-success-secrets.com/statistics-about-children-and-divorce.html.

[43] Proverbs 22:6, Amplified Bible.

[44] Exodus 34:7.

[45] Isaiah 43:19, NLT.

[46] Matthew 6:15 NLT.

[47] Isaiah 1:18.

[48] Psalm 103:12.

[49] Ann Voskamp, http://www.aholyexperience.com/ann-voskamp/.

[50] *Shunning within the Amish Community in Lancaster County: The Practice of Social Avoidance*, http://www.welcome-to-lancaster-county.com/amish-community.html.

[51] *The Hands Of A Woman: Everyday Women In Everyday Battles*, Beth Jones, Refreshing Waters Ministry, Butler, MO, http://womensbattles.com.

[52] *The Therapeutic Relationship As The Foundation For Treatment With Adult Survivors of Sexual Abuse*, Karen A. Olio and William F. Cornell, http://kspope.com/memory/relationship.php.

[53] *The High Cost of Sexual Abuse Recovery*, Vicki Messer, http://www.associatedcontent.com/article/683099/the_high_cost_of_keeping_the_family_pg3.html?cat=72.

[54] Ibid.

[55] Ibid.

[56] *Amish Shunning*, http://www.exploring-amish-country.com/amish-shunning.html.

[57] *Fiddler On the Roof*, Norman Jewison, 1971, http://www.imdb.com/title/tt0067093/.

[58] *Amish Shunning*, http://www.exploring-amish-country.com/amish-shunning.html.

[59] *Tom Cruise Admits Katie Holmes Divorced Him To Protect Suri From Scientology*, Huffington Post, http://www.huffingtonpost.com/2013/11/08/tom-cruise-katie-holmes-protect-suri-scientology_n_4240715.html

[60] *Amish Shunning*, http://www.exploring-amish-country.com/amish-shunning.html.

[61] *Cleaning the Leper*, Hampton Keathley IV, http://bible.org/seriespage/cleansing-leper.

[62] Ibid.

[63] Ibid.

[64] Mark 1:40-45.

[65] *Biblical Leprosy: Shedding Light on the Disease that Shuns*, Alan L. Gillen, Ed.D., 2007, http://www.answersingenesis.org/articles/am/v2/n3/the-disease-that-shuns.

[66] 2 Corinthians 5:18.

[67] John 10:10, NLT.

[68] John 16:33.

[69] *A Scarlett Cord of Hope*, Sheryl Griffin, Westview, Inc., 2009, p. 128.

[70] Genesis Chapters 37-45.

[71] John 10:10.

[72] Genesis 1:31.

[73] Genesis 3.

[74] Luke 19:41-44.

[75] *A Bible Study on Becoming a Woman of Love*, Cynthia Heald, Thomas Nelson, Inc., Nashville, TN, © 2002, p. 99.)

[76] *I Know Why The Caged Bird Sings*, Maya Angelou, Ballantine Books, New York, © 2009, pp. 70-84.)

[77] *Everything*, Mary E. DeMuth, Thomas Nelson, © 2012, pp. 25-26.

[78] *Effects of Child Abuse on Children*, http://www.findcounseling.com/journal/child-abuse/child-abuse-effects.html

[79] *Everything*, Mary E. DeMuth, Thomas Nelson, © 2012, p. 97.

[80] *Stormie: A Story of Forgiveness and Healing*, Stormie O'Martian, Harvest House Publishers, Eugene, OR, 1986, pp. 185-188.

[81] Psalm 107:19-21.

[82] *The Scarlett Letter*, Nathaniel Hawthorne, Ticknor, Reed & Fields, 1850.

[83] *Fatal Attraction*, Adrian Lyne, 1987, http://www.imdb.com/title/tt0093010/.

[84] *Consequences of Adultery*, Christ Church (EPC) Men's Blog, http://christchurchepc.wordpress.com/2009/10/07/consequences-of-adultery/.

[85] Blasphemy is the only unforgiveable sin, which Jesus talked about in Matthew 12:31-32.

[86] *The Ex-Abortionists: Why They Quit*, The Human Life Foundation, Inc., New York, NY, 2012, http://www.cogforlife.org/abortionquitters.htm.

[87] Ibid.

[88] Ibid.

[89] *Post Abortion Syndrome Symptoms*, Sydna Masse' Blog, Ramah International, Fayetteville, AR, http://www.ramahinternational.org/post-abortion-syndrome-symptoms.html.

[90] Ibid.

[91] *Women Who Have Abortions*, National Federation Fact Sheet, http://www.prochoice.org/about_abortion/facts/women_who.html.

[92] *Gianna Jessen Abortion Survivor in Australia Part 1*, TelltheTruthTv, YouTube, http://www.youtube.com/watch?v=kPF1FhCMPuQ.

[93] Ibid.

[94] *Gift From The Sea*, Anne Morrow Lindbergh, Pantheon, © January 30, 1991.

[95] *Possible Physical Side Effects*, http://americanpregnancy.org/unplannedpregnancy/possiblesideeffects.html

[96] *Information on Domestic Violence*, http://www.domesticabuseshelter.org/InfoDomesticViolence.htm.

[97] Exodus 20:1-18.

[98] Diederich, F. Remy (2011-11-27). *Healing the Hurts of Your Past: A Guide to Overcoming the Pain of Shame* (Kindle Locations 1541-1542). Cross Point Publishing. Kindle Edition.

[99] Ibid.

[100] *The Hands Of A Woman: Everyday Women In Everyday Battles*, http://womensbattles.com.

[101] *The Strange Case of Dr. Jekyll and Mr. Hyde and Other Tales of Terror*, Robert Louis Stevens, http://www.amazon.com/The-Strange-Case-Jekyll-Hyde/dp/0141439734.

[102] *Harvest of Hope: Living Victoriously Through Adversity*, Dana Arcuri, 2014, p. 100.

[103] *Addiction by Prescription: One Woman's Triumph and Fight for Change*, Joan E. Gadsby, Key Porter Books, March 1, 2000.

[104] Ibid, p. 77.

[105] Ibid, p. 79.

[106] Ibid, p. 98.

[107] Ibid, p. 100.

[108] *Former Abortion Clinic Worker Describes Seeing Body Parts of Aborted Babies*, http://www.lifenews.com/2014/03/24/former-abortion-clinic-worker-describes-seeing-body-parts-of-aborted-babies/.

[109] *Stronger*, Kelly Clarkson, RCA Records, a Division of Sony Music Entertainment, http://www.youtube.com/watch?v=Xn676-fLq7I.

[110] 1 John 1:9.

[111] Isaiah 1:8, NIV.

[112] Proverbs 13:25, NASB.

[113] *Hinds' Feet On High Places*, Mrs. Darien B. Cooper and Hannah Hurnard, Destiny Image, Resissue Feb. 19, 2013, http://www.amazon.com/Hinds-Feet-High-Places-Devotional/dp/0768442028.

[114] John 6:35.

[115] Acts 17:28.

[116] 1 Corinthians 7:23.

[117] Proverbs 1:5.

[118] Psalm 139:14.

[119] Psalm 139:16-18.

[120] James 2:8-9.

[121] John 10:10, CEV.

[122] Matthew 10:29-31.

[123] Psalm 111:10.

[124] This is not my first husband's real name. Some pseudonyms are used throughout this book, but the facts are real.

[125] "Todd" is not his real name, but a pseudonym. Some pseudonyms are used throughout this book, but the facts are real.

[126] Matthew 10:29.

[127] Jeremiah 18.

[128] *What Can Happen to Abused Children When They Grow Up – If No One Notices, Listens or Helps,* Office of Trauma Services, Maine Department of Behavioral and Developmental Services, Augsta, ME, http://www.theannainstitute.org/wchac-stats.html..

[129] Ibid.

[130] Ibid.

[131] *Captivating, Unveiling The Mystery of a Woman's Soul,* John and Stasi Eldredge, Thomas Nelson Publishers, July 10, 2007, http://www.amazon.com/Captivating-Unveiling-Mystery-Womans-Soul-ebook/dp/B006ID035K.

[132] Proverbs 5:21-23.

[133] Dr. Phil, *Dangerous Online Obsession,* September 18, 2013, http://drphil.com/shows/show/2066.

[134] *Statistics About Affairs,* Peggy Vaughan, Extramarital Affairs Resource Center, http://www.dearpeggy.com/2-affairs/statistics.html.

[135] *Sleepless in Seattle,* Nora Ephron, 1993, http://en.wikipedia.org/wiki/Sleepless_in_Seattle.

[136] Psalm 56:8-11, NLV.

[137] Proverbs 5:3-5.

[138] James 5:16, The Message Bible.

[139] *Affairs in the Workplace,* http://www.myeasttexaspi.com/workplace_affairs.htm.

[140] 1 Corinthians 10:12.

[141] Proverbs 6:12, NIV.

[142] *When A Woman Finds Her Voice,* Jo Ann Fore, Leafwood Publishers, Albilene, TX, 2013, p. 15.

[143] Exodus 34:6-7, The Message.

[144] "Hakuna Matata," *The Lion King*, http://www.youtube.com/watch?v=xB5ceAruYrI,

[145] 1 Peter 1:16.

[146] 1 Corinthians 10:12, Living Bible.

[147] Genesis 39.

[148] Matthew 19:26.

[149] *Project: Happily Ever After*, Alisa Bowman, Running Press Book Publishers, Philadelphia, PA, 2010, pp. 106-107.

[150] Ibid.

[151] Ruth Bell and Billy Graham Marriage Profile, http://marriage.about.com/od/celebritymarriages/p/billgraham.htm, Source: Jon Meacham. "Pilgrim's Progress." *Newsweek*. 8/14/2006, pg. 36.

[152] *The War of the Roses*, December 8, 1989, http://www.imdb.com/title/tt0098621/.

[153] *Mars and Venus: Communication Styles of Men and Women*, Alexandra Zatarain, http://www.css-llc.net/blog/mars-and-venus-communication-styles-of-men-and-women/.

[154] *Six Ways Men and Women Communicate Differently*, Richard Drobnick, http://psychcentral.com/blog/archives/2012/04/01/6-ways-men-and-women-communicate-differently/.

[155] Lamentations 3:22-23.

[156] Divorce statistics, http://www.divorcestatistics.org/.

157 *Under the Tuscan Sun*, Director Audrey Wells, http://www.imdb.com/title/tt0328589/.

158 *This Isn't the Life I Signed Up For*, Donna Partow, Bethany House Publishers, Bloomington, MN, 2003.

159 *Love Life For Every Married Couple: How to Fall In Love and Stay in Love*, Ed Wheat, M.D., and Gloria Okes Perkins, Harpers Collins Publishers, New York, NY, 1989, p. 152.

160 Revelation 19:11.

161 2 Corinthians 1:20.

162 Psalm 119: 89.

163 Deuteronomy 37:29.

164 Isaiah 54:5.

165 Deuteronomy 31:16, The Message.

166 John 5:1-8.

167 Isaiah 54:5.

168 Psalm 56:8.

169 Revelation 12:11, NLV.

170 John 10:27-28, The Message.

171 *A Series of Unfortunate Events,* http://en.wikipedia.org/wiki/A_Series_of_Unfortunate_Events.

[172] *How Many Bible Promises Are There?*, http://www.bibleinfo.com/en/questions/how-many-bible-promises-are-there.

[173] *God's promise to Abraham*, http://www.bigbiblechallenge.com/gods-promise-to-abraham/.

[174] 2 Corinthians 1:20.

[175] Numbers 23:19.

[176] Genesis 18:1-12.

[177] Psalm 2:4.

[178] Ephesians 3:20, The Message.

# Resources

**The Bible.** This is the greatest resource I know for life, relationships, spiritual, mental, emotional, and physical health, finances, success, and business. I love God's word!

## Business

### Beth Jones, International Speaker/Author/Coach –
Keynote women's conference and event speaker, http://www.bethjones.net/speaking/

Coaching packages to help you succeed in life and in business- www.bethjones.net/coaching/packages. When I travel and speak at live events, I feel most alive and energized. It is what God created me to do and to be. I love God's daughters and encouraging them to fulfill their great purpose and fullest potential!

### Rochelle Valasek, Speaker/Author/Coach, http://www.rochellevalasek.com.
Rochelle, aka "Shelley," is my speaking coach, my very precious friend, my mastermind, prayer and accountability partner. Shelley has God the Father's huge heart of love, mercy and compassion. She has been through one fiery trial after another, including a nearly fatal car accident, but God has preserved her life to fulfill her great purpose and she has kept her faith in Christ strong through it all. She's one of the most anointed speakers I've ever heard. You'll be greatly blessed by meeting her. Shelley also is a consultant for doTerra Essential Oils, a product for healthy living that you'll just love. (My faves are frankincense and lavender!)

**Tony Robinson, Speaker/Author/Coach//Minister/ Missionary**, http://wellwateredwoman.com/. Tony is my mastermind, prayer, and accountability partner, and my dear friend. She hears clearly from the Lord in prayer and God has used her many times to prophesy God's truth and abundant life into my spirit and into many other women's lives across the globe. She's a powerhouse speaker and minister for God, who will bless your women's event over and above your expectations.

**Doreen Penner, Speaker/Author/Coach**, http://www.doreenpenner.com. Doreen is my weekly prayer and accountability partner. She has been a breath of fresh air and a source of continual encouragement to me on this entrepreneurial online journey. Doreen is one of the most polished speakers I've ever seen, and as a coach, she will help you to get to the heart of the matter with her wise insights and loving yet challenging words. She prayed continually for my book to be finished — like the "sail" on a sailboat in rough ocean waters for me to get safely to the shore.

**NACWE** – National Association of Christian Women Entrepreneurs, Diane Cunningham's organization to help Christian women succeed in business. www.nacwe.org. If you join, I'd really appreciate you using my affiliate link on this page. Just scroll down until you see the graphic and click on it. http://www.bethjones.net/my-fave-things/. Please tell Diane I referred you to her! I love that beautiful woman of God! As a leader, entrepreneur, a coach and former boss, and a biz peer, she has greatly inspired me. Diane's passion and fire for God, brilliance, creativity, and encouragement have been used by God to be instrumental in giving me hope that I can achieve great success with my online business, too.

**Dana Arcuri, Speaker/Author/Plexus Slim Consultant**, http://www.danaarcuri.com. Dana was my coaching client, hiring me in 2013, to motivate her to finish writing her powerful memoir,

*Harvest of Hope: Living Victoriously Through Adversity*. Since then she has been running with the vision God has given her, writing, speaking, selling her book, coaching, and being greatly blessed using and promoting/selling Plexus Slim online. She's an anointed woman of God, who will greatly encourage you and give you hope through sharing her personal story of triumph and her persevering faith in Jesus Christ.

**Jo Ann Fore, Speaker/Author/Coach**, http://www.joannfore.com/. Jo Ann writes beautifully, and her writings and encouragement have inspired me in my own writing journey. You'll find stories of hope and healing for childhood sexual abuse and other traumas at her website, and her Write Where It Hurts online community. She encourages others to use the powerful tool of journaling to heal and move forward.

# Health

**Donna Partow, Speaker/Author/Coach**, http://www.donnapartow.com. I've read several of Donna's books (and plan to buy more!) and was a student in her 90-Day Renewal online group class beginning in January 2014. Donna is an anointed speaker, writer and coach who will be the kick in the butt you need for seeking God first, weight loss/fitness, and emotional/spiritual health.

# Suicide Prevention

## American Foundation for Suicide Prevention
http://www.afsp.org
1-800-273-8255

## Canadian Association for Suicide Prevention (CASP)
http://www.suicideprevention.ca/

## Suicide Hotlines
http://www.suicide.org/suicide-hotlines.html

# Mental Health

## Lucy Ann Moll, Christian Biblical Counselor, pastor's wife and Co-Founder of Grace Life Church, Sycamore, Illinois.
I have personally used Lucy Ann for crisis counseling. She's a Biblically-based, anointed counselor who speaks the truth in love, gives wise counseling, and prays for you, whatever your need is. I highly recommend her. You can do the counseling over Skype, which is very convenient. http://www.lucyannmoll.com/

## Karen Wells, Individual, Marriage & Family Therapist Karis Counselling Services, Canada (Skype counseling)
http://www.mybestlifepossible.com/. Karen is a friend and a business peer and I highly recommend her as a therapist, a speaker, and a coach. She is biblically-based, wise and discerning, and will tell you the truth, giving you practical advice, effective tools and resources, and encouraging scriptures to help you heal from past trauma, hurts, and relationship difficulties.

## Benzodiazepine Support Group—An online forum
to connect with others experiencing similar challenges with benzodiazepines. http://www.benzobuddies.org/forum/index.php

# Spiritual Gifts

***The Gifts and Ministries of the Holy Spirit* by Lester Sumrall,** http://www.amazon.com/Gifts-Ministries-Spirit-SUMRALL-LESTER/dp/0883682362/ref=sr_1_1?s=books&ie=UTF8&qid=1400538527&sr=1-1&keywords=the+gifts+and+ministries+of+the+holy+spirit+by+lester+sumrall.

The best book I've read for explaining the definition, the purpose, and the practical use of each of the spiritual gifts.

***Step Out and Take Your Place* by Krista Dunk,** http://www.stepoutandtakeyourplace.com/buyresources.htm.

This is the most comprehensive book I've ever read on the spiritual gifts, God's calling for your life, and your purpose.

# Prayer and Contemporary Worship/Praise

**K-Love Radio Station,** http://www.klove.com/ministry/prayer/ 800-525-5683

# Promises In The Dark

# About the Author

**Beth Jones** is an International Speaker/Author/ Coach, wife of twenty-one years to paramedic Ray Jones, and mom of three beautiful daughters, Heather, Eden, and Leah. She is passionate about women fulfilling their purpose and seeing their big dreams come true through exercising bold faith in Christ. Beth's life scripture and calling are Isaiah 61, to set the captives free. Her mission is equipping women to use their spiritual gifts for God's glory, doing what they love, and prospering in all areas of life.

Beth resides in the Kansas City, Missouri area. You can find out more about her women's conference keynote speaking at www.BethJones.net. Her signature talk about women walking in their incredible destiny is *The Power of Shoes*, based on the story of Cinderella.

As soon as she takes the stage, you can feel Beth's sincere devotion to Jesus Christ. Her direct, "tell-the-truth-like-it-is" style, combined with a heart of compassion and humor, appeal to audiences large or small. The two most frequent words used to describe Beth's speaking presentations are "intense" and "real."

Speaking and traveling are Beth's favorite things to do. She travels nationally and internationally for speaking engagements. She is easy to work with, loves connecting with and praying with each woman (not speaking and just running off!), and will answer the audience's questions, autograph books, and take pictures with staff and attendees. Had a speaker cancel at the last minute? Beth can fill in as your speaker, if her schedule allows.

Beth loves Jesus, her family, chocolate, Mexican food, horses, nature, art, music, reading, Sharpie ultra-fine pens, comfy pjs, and cute new shoes. Her husband Ray calls her an "enigma." She loves to laugh and cries a lot.

To contact Beth, email her at elizabethdjones@gmail.com or visit her at www.BethJones.net.

www.ingramcontent.com/pod-product-compliance
Lightning Source LLC
Chambersburg PA
CBHW071910290426
44110CB00013B/1346